# Behavior Modeling Training for Developing Supervisory Skills

## Instructor Manual

# Behavior Modeling Training for Developing Supervisory Skills

## Instructor Manual

by

William M. Fox, PhD

IAP

Information Age Publishing, Inc.
Charlotte, North Carolina • www.infoagepub.com

ISBN: 978-1-59311-981-2



Printed in the United States of America

# CONTENTS

Preface ........ ix

**Part I: The Nature and Strengths of Behavior Modeling** ........ 1
Evidence of Effectiveness ........ 1
Background Overview of Supporting Theory ........ 2
  Attentional Processes ........ 3
  Retention Processes ........ 3
  Motor Reproduction Processes ........ 3
  Motivational Processes ........ 3
The Basic Components ........ 3
  Learning Points ........ 3
  Demonstration ........ 4
    Attributes of the Model and Modeling Situation ........ 4
    Advantages of an In-House Demonstration Videotape ........ 5
    Possible Refinements ........ 5
  Trainee Practice With Feedback ........ 5
    Assignment to Roleplay Groups ........ 6
    Needed Rolesets ........ 6
    Mental Rehearsal ........ 6
    Feedback ........ 6
    Use of Videotape Playback ........ 7
  Follow-Up ........ 7
    The Need For Overlearning ........ 7
    The Need For On-the-Job Practice and Remedial Action ........ 7
Acceptability to Trainees ........ 7
Background Overview of Applications ........ 8
  First Written Presentation ........ 8
  Use of in World War I ........ 8
  Use of in World War II ........ 9
  Other Uses ........ 9
Notes ........ 9
Appendix: Examples of Learning-Point Modules ........ 13
  Nonjudgmental Information Gathering ........ 13
  Remedial Action ........ 14

When Person Fails to Properly Implement a Remedial-Action Program . . . . . 14
Giving Recognition . . . . . 14
Handling A Complaining Employee . . . . . 14
Delegating Work . . . . . 15
Handling Insubordination . . . . . 15
Reducing Absenteeism . . . . . 15
Improving Safety Habits . . . . . 15
Conducting A Performance-Review Interview . . . . . 15
Mediating Between Conflicting Individuals . . . . . 15
Short Form for Supervisors to Use With Two Subordinates During a Meeting of the Three . . . . . 16
Basic Learning Points for Many One-on-One Modules . . . . . 16

**PART II: Conduct of the Training** . . . . . 17
Preparing for the First Practice Session . . . . . 17
Selecting the First Trainees . . . . . 17
Assigning the Trainees to Groups . . . . . 17
Needed Resources . . . . . 17
Prepractice Activity . . . . . 20
The First Practice Session . . . . . 20
Phase One Activity . . . . . 20
Lead Discussion of the Learning Points . . . . . 20
Discussion of the Nonjudgmental Information Gathering Learning Points . . . . . 21
Discussion of the Remedial Action Learning Points . . . . . 21
Show the Modeling Demonstration . . . . . 22
(Optional) After Reaching Agreement . . . . . 23
Phase Two Activity . . . . . 23
Phase Three Activity . . . . . 23
Possible Comments, Questions, and Answers . . . . . 23
Homework Assignment . . . . . 24
Overlearning Practice for Some . . . . . 25
The Follow-Up Meeting . . . . . 25
Stimulating and Maintaining a Felt Need for Training . . . . . 25
Formal Evaluation of Training . . . . . 26
Collecting "Before" and "After" Samples for Trainees Who Have Subordinates . . . . . 26

Collecting "Before" and "After" Samples for Trainees Who Do Not Have Subordinates . . . 26
Study End-of-Practice-Session Data . . . 27
Forms Provided in the Trainee-Manual Appendix . . . 27
Notes . . . 27

**Appendix A: All Forms . . . 29**
Learning Points Worksheet . . . 30
Roleplay Input Form . . . 32
Observer Form . . . 33
Homework Assignment Sheet . . . 35
Learning Points Refresher Sheet . . . 36
End-of-Practice-Session Questionnaire . . . 37
Questionnaire A . . . 38
Questionnaire B . . . 40

**Appendix B: Rolesets for Four-Person Groups . . . 43**
Roleset for Group Member W . . . 44
Roleset for Group Member X . . . 47
Roleset for Group Member Y . . . 50
Roleset for Group Member Z . . . 53

**Appendix C: Rolesets for Three-Person Groups . . . 57**
Roleset for Group Member T . . . 58
Roleset for Group Member U . . . 60
Roleset for Group Member V . . . 62

# Preface

Behavior modeling has been a highly successful training method for centuries. However, refinements based on extensive research about its components began only recently. This manual presents the fruits of this research, and provides hands-on, proven, detailed instructions for productive implementation.

It is designed to be used in conjunction with *Behavior Modeling Training for Developing Supervisory Skills: Trainee Manual* by this author, which contains multiple copies of various forms that the trainee will use.

# Part I

# The Nature and Strengths of Behavior Modeling Training

Behavior modeling* is a form of skill-development training that is distinguished by the manner in which it integrates essential "knowledge about" and "experience with." It has been used successfully to train supervisors in:

- conducting performance reviews,
- correcting inadequate performance,
- delegating work,
- handling insubordination,
- handling a subordinate's complaint,
- reducing absenteeism,
- improving safety habits,
- handling racial discrimination complaints,
- reducing resentment toward female supervisors,
- overcoming resistance to change,
- orienting new employees,
- mediating between conflicting individuals or groups, and
- utilizing survey feedback data collaboratively with subordinates.

And other supervisory applications may be readily developed. The skills learned help supervisors create fairer and less threatening work environments that produce better output and enhance the self-esteem and loyalty of subordinates.

Behavior modeling has also been effective as a training mode in athletics, medicine, the theater, selling, and various vocational and other skills. In addition, it is an effective tool for helping individuals to overcome inhibitions or emotional blocks to such activities as handling distasteful objects, giving praise, or making assertive statements.

Though the demands made on the trainee by the two aspects of learning ("knowledge about" and "skillful doing") vary considerably across these examples, the differences can be easily accommodated by the design and execution of the behavior-modeling components. For example, in dealing with inhibitions to needed assertiveness or the giving of deserved praise, the knowledge component is largely self-evident (the trainee already "knows" what he or she should do), so more emphasis is given to the "doing" phase.

## Evidence of Effectiveness

The results from numerous studies with diverse groups of trainees, indicate that behavior modeling—

*In addition to the term "behavior modeling," all, or some, elements of the same approach have been identified by other terms such as: applied learning, behavior modeling-interaction management (BMIM), behavioral rehearsal, behavioral replications technique, behavioral training, interactive modeling, interpersonal skills training, job instruction training (JIT), managerial skills training, social skills training, structured learning therapy, and supervisory relationships training. Apparently, the term "behavior modeling" did not appear before the 1970s.

when properly used—provides the most effective approach yet developed for skill-development training. For example, Falcone, Edwards, and Day used sophisticated statistical analysis (meta-analysis) to assess the results of skills training for supervisors, nonsupervisors, and students that were produced by several training techniques: sensitivity training (63 studies), behavior modeling (21 studies), programmed instruction (18 studies), computer-assisted instruction (five studies), and programmed instruction coupled with computer assisted instruction (22 studies). Clearly, behavior modeling was the most effective technique overall. And a meta-analysis of 97 studies by Paul Taylor found it to be effective in a variety of cross-cultural locations.[1]

Jon Werner and Suzanne Crampton selected 13 studies on cognitive-skill training—from a larger group of 60 potentially relevant studies—that were suitable for meta-analysis. They found that behavior modeling was significantly effective on both a behavioral criterion (ability to apply the new cognitive skills in a non-modeled-situation roleplay) and a results criterion (appraised on-the-job performance).[2] Lastly, the author found strong, significant effects for behavior-modeling training in his review of 44 single-skill-area training studies and 14 multiple-module, supervisory-skills, training studies. Only five of these were associated with weak or missing effects.

Behavior modeling provides properly guided experience. To appreciate the value of this approach, one need only reflect on what we all must do to master activities such as dancing, driving a car, or making a presentation. We must go beyond merely reading about, hearing about, or observing the techniques involved; we must add guided practice, feedback, and adjusted practice. The omission of one or more of these components produces poorer results.

In addition, the reporting of poor results may be caused by inadequate "before-training" and "after-training" behavior sampling. Epstein found that correlations between single observations of expectedly similar behavior rarely exceed .30, even when one takes into account the interaction of the person with the situation. However, he found good stability for self-recorded data, observations of overt behavior, and direct measurements of objective behavior, when at least five or six behavior samples were taken over a period of time—in comparable situations—and then aggregated.[3]

Furthermore, when the impact on output is an effectiveness criterion, evaluators need to keep in mind that positive changes in subordinate performance may lag positive changes in the behavior of their supervisors by several months to several years—the more prevalent time frame being 7-16 months. And, often, a transitional drop in subordinate performance occurs before improvement.[4]

Another criterion, the immediate, posttraining perceptions by subordinates of changes in their supervisor's behavior, may be misleading, because opportunity to use the new skills with sufficient frequency has not yet occurred. For example, Sorcher and Spence found much stronger posttraining results after 14 weeks than after 6 weeks.[5] Also, it may take time for the newly trained supervisor to perfect the use of the new skills. Burnaska found that trainees performed better on blindly evaluated roleplays 4 months after training than they did immediately after training.[6]

## Background Overview of Supporting Theory

Early proponents of behavior modeling failed to provide any supporting theory. They were pragmatists—the approach was intuitively appealing, and it worked. Viteles and others reported various findings about the processes of learning as they became available, but they did not acknowledge the behavior-modeling paradigm, let alone theorize about it.[7]

Rosenthal[8] suggests that the earliest speculation about behavior modeling was of a behaviorist bent; however, limitations to such an explanation became apparent in 1920, when Hull demonstrated that the presentation of concept examples was as efficient as trial-and-error learning—that acquisition required neither reinforcement nor direct task practice, though both, together, outperformed either, alone. And he cites numerous subsequent studies which imply that human learning is grounded primarily in central information processing events, rather than simply on associative bonds that join overt stimuli and responses.[9]

Albert Bandura took such findings and coupled them with the fruits of his own research to formulate social learning theory—the most fully developed theoretical model we currently have for behavior modeling. His first comprehensive presentation of the theory was made in 1977.[10] Then, in 1986, he expanded on it with additional supporting data.[11]

Bandura asserts that the larger part of human behavior is learned through the observation of others (models), and that such observational learning is governed by four processes. The subparts presented below are those that are most relevant to supervisory skills training:

### Attentional Processes

These processes regulate sensory registration of the modeled actions, with particular relevance to:

- the characteristics of the observer,
- the characteristics of the model,
- the functional value of the behavior to the observer, and
- the salience and complexity of the observed behavior.

### Retention Processes

Whereby transitory influences are converted to enduring internal guides for memory representation. Visual or verbal retention is affected by:

- intensity and repetition,
- coding by the observer to summarize and organize observed behavior, and
- mental rehearsal.

### Motor Reproduction Processes

Whereby symbolic representations are converted into appropriate action. They involve:

- the cognitive organization of responses,
- initiation (constrained by the observer's possession of component skills),
- monitoring (including awareness of kinesthetic cues), and
- refinement on the basis of goal-related feedback.

### Motivational Processes

These determine whether or not acquired responses will be converted to overt behavior. Of particular relevance are:

- The observed consequences (both intrinsic and extrinsic) of the observed behavior,
- the compatibility of the observed behavior with the style preferences of the observer, and
- the observer's self-management (for example, his or her reinforcement of self for measured progress against self-set goals).

Bandura asserts that creative behavior results from the synthesis of information from various models and/or mediation by the observer's style. His social learning theory explains human behavior in terms of a continuous, reciprocal interaction between cognitive, behavioral, and environmental determinants. It asserts that although reinforcement provides an effective means for regulation of behavior that has already been learned, it is a relatively inefficient means for creating new behavior. Based on his review of relevant studies, Saltz shares this conclusion.[12]

Along with Saltz and others, Bandura also asserts that attitude change is not the most effective means for inducing changes in overt behavior, that, generally, the opposite linkage—the impact of overt behavior upon attitudes—is stronger.[13] A review of the literature by Triandis provides reasons for this weakness of the attitude-overt-behavior linkage. He found no less than 40 variables which can moderate the relationship (14 methodological and 26 substantive).[14]

## The Basic Components

There are four basic behavior-modeling components:

- learning points (instructions) for mastering a skill,
- demonstration of the skill by a competent model,
- trainee practice with feedback, and
- follow-up remedial action and reinforcement to encourage sustained mastery and transfer to non-training settings.

### Learning Points

According to Bandura's theory of observational learning, the process of trainee symbolization that is prompted by demonstration modeling is greatly facilitated by the trainee's ability to attach verbal labels to the modeled behavior. In addition, such symbolic coding facilitates retention of the transitory modeling experience.[15]

Decker and others have found support for these assertions. They have demonstrated that the inclusion of learning points enhances behavior-modeling training.[16] In addition, Decker and others have shown that learning points for developing cognitive-type skills are most effective in the form of rule/goal-oriented guidelines, because this format encourages trainees to recreate modeled behavior in various situations with their own personal style, rather than simply attempting to imitate demonstrated behavior.[17] In addition, specific, subgoals provide motivation to act, and learning points constitute behavioral subgoals.[18]

It should be noted, however, that for precisely prescribed motor skills (such as operating a power tool or performing a delicate medical operation), learning points like those in this manual (that present principles or goals to be satisfied) are not as productive as those that encourage trainees to mimic modeled behavior.[19]

The appendix to Part I presents examples of various learning-point modules (sets of learning points) that have been used successfully for developing supervisory skills. Other modules can be developed as the need arises. They should be grounded in authoritative consensus on the part of those who have experienced first-hand knowledge of the activity and the particular setting (or settings) in which the activity occurs (or will occur), and be developed according to the additional guidelines presented below.

The choice of learning points for initial behavior-modeling training should be based on an assessment of current supervisory-skills deficits. Among useful ways to determine these:

- Solicit input from present supervisors as to the situations that challenge them most in dealing with subordinates, or ask in what areas they would most like to receive training.
- Check the nature of employee-inputted grievances and suggestions.
- Look at the nature of reported, interpersonal-relations deficiencies in the performance ratings of supervisors.
- Solicit anonymous input from employees as to what their supervisors should:
    - start doing,
    - stop doing,
    - do less of,
    - do more of,
    - do differently.

Once need is established, a useful tool for developing new learning-point modules—or for refining old ones—is the Critical Incident Technique (CIT) of job analysis.[20] It requires that those who are knowledgeable about the activity describe, independently, specific examples of effective and ineffective performance.

Also, research findings show that learning points can be more readily handled by trainees when no more than eight are placed in a given module.[21] If more are needed, additional modules should be created.

With regard to all learning points, the most effective ones are manageable, credible, and understandable to the trainee. Decker has shown that a useful first step is to invite trainees to examine them to determine their meaning and to identify possible ambiguities or other deficiencies; then, to accept proposed revisions in wording that do not alter their basic intent.[22] We may infer support for this approach, also, from persuasive evidence about the importance of understandability and acceptance in effective goal setting.[23]

## Demonstration

In accordance with Bandura's social learning theory, outcome expectations and self-efficacy expectations (assumed ability to execute a behavior) are enhanced by the vicarious experience of observing successful execution by a model, accompanied or followed by positive consequences.

Research findings support this theory. They have demonstrated the superiority of learning points with modeling, versus learning points without modeling.[24] And modeling, alone, has significantly influenced the modification of social withdrawal in children;[25] assertiveness in adults;[26] independent behavior on the part of adult psychiatric outpatients;[27] empathic communication on the part of college students;[28] and success in desensitization therapy, the treatment of test anxiety, and the treatment of various phobias.[29] In addition, a meta-analysis by Shapiro and Shapiro of therapy outcomes yielded a significant role for modeling.[30]

However, as one might expect, when training need is largely one of disinhibition for known or very simple responses (such as learning to be more assertive), modeling, as well as learning points, do not play the uniquely important roles that they play in training for complex, new knowledge and/or skill acquisition.[31]

By way of contrast, traditional-roleplaying training is generally less effective than properly executed behavior-modeling training, due to the absence of appropriate learning points and prepractice modeling. Typically, it does not provide trainees with the same level of appropriate guidance and confidence when they begin their roleplays. Consequently, they often finish with greater frustration and diminished feelings of self-efficacy.

### *Attributes of the Model and Modeling Situation*

There is clear evidence that the characteristics of the model and the modeling situation affect how strongly the demonstrated behaviors will be attended to and acquired, and the likelihood that the new behaviors will be implemented in non-training situations. The following are model attributes that have been found to be most effective for the demonstration of cognitive skills. The model:

- has high status and credibility (high expertise and/or trustworthiness) in the eyes of the trainees,
- controls resources desired by them,
- is of the same sex and race as they, is apparently friendly and helpful, and
- is rewarded in a way that is important to them, for engaging in the prescribed behaviors.[32]

In this regard, John Paulsen, a highly successful trainer with IBM, related the following to the author to underscore the importance of proper "casting." He and his associates had recruited models from a manufacturing plant in the mid-South with whom they had successfully developed a series of modeling videotapes for use in a training program at the plant. The taped performances were well-received there. But when they were used for training same-company managers in New York City, the models proved to be unacceptable, despite the fact that the learning points were quite acceptable. Apparently, the New York managers were "turned off" by the accents or other attractiveness attributes of the southern models.

In addition, there is evidence that the more that the modeling situation and setting are like the situation(s) and setting(s) in which we desire the modeled behaviors to be used, the more likely that the training will have an impact, and will be transferred to the job.[33] However, to the extent that a given group of trainees represents diverse organizations and settings, a demonstration that presents a more "neutral" model performing in a more "neutral" roleplay setting may be the most suitable.

### *Advantages of an In-House Demonstration Videotape*

What about the effectiveness of "live" versus taped modeling? Research evidence indicates that taped modeling demonstrations are just as effective,[34] so there is no point in foregoing the advantages of constant model availability, consistently correct enactment, and convenience. In addition, taping makes it more feasible to have a high-ranking member of an organization add to the trainees' motivation to learn, by introducing what they are about to see and explaining why it is important for them to master what is being presented.

Taping also makes it possible to produce a copy of the modeling tape for a second showing with the learning points presented (and/or narrated) with the scenes in which they are utilized. In the first showing (without the learning points) trainees should be asked to record where they occur in the enactment on a worksheet (see the *Learning Points Worksheet* in Appendix A of Part II). After discussion of the worksheet results, the second version of the tape can be shown to provide additional feedback and reinforcement as to proper learning-point usage.

To make a modeling tape that will be most credible for the trainees, solicit input from them as to challenging situations they have encountered that relate to the activity of the learning-point module to be demonstrated. Useful ideas can be solicited by means such as the *Roleplay Input Form* presented in Appendix A of Part II. The role descriptions should be presented in the same manner as those presented in the rolesets in Appendixes B and C of Part II.

For reasons presented earlier, the language and physical setting for the modeling tape should be the same as those which the trainees are accustomed to. Ideally, when trainees are from the same organization, the person playing the supervisor should be a respected, in-house manager. With regard to cost, a good generalization is that authenticity is more important than "slickness" of the production.

### *Possible Refinements*

Concept and problem-solving research findings suggest that stimulus variability can improve both trainee retention and skill application to different settings.[35] One form of this involves varying the modeling situation; for example, demonstrating a given learning-point module with a cooperative employee, and then with a difficult, hostile employee. Bandura and Menlove found that the observance of different models with different dogs was more effective in reducing avoidance behavior than observance of a single model with a single dog.[36] And Sechrest found that several different examples, repeated a few times, enhanced learning more than the repeated presentation of one example.[37]

Another type of stimulus variability is the presentation of both positive and negative (wrong way) modeling, so that knowledge of the correct way is enhanced by an opportunity to compare it with same-situation incorrect ways.[38] However, a possible disadvantage is that this may not facilitate transfer of the skill as fast to a job situation that is identical with the modeling situation.

## TRAINEE PRACTICE WITH FEEDBACK

Research findings support the common-sense observation that instructions alone are not sufficient for skill development—hands-on practice is also required.[39]

For cognitive-skills training, as opposed to motor-skills training (such as as for learning to type or perform a routine machine-maintenance function), we want trainees to be their authentic selves in applying the learning points in their rehearsal roleplays. We do not want them merely to mimic the behavior of the model. Therefore, trainees should be supplied with rule- or goal-oriented learning points (like those presented in the Appendix) and, for optimal transfer of learning, with roleplay situations that have occurred, or are likely to occur, in-house, should the trainees be from the same organization.

### *Assignment to Roleplay Groups*

Prior to the first practice session, trainees should be assigned to groups of three or, preferably, four. Small groups are desirable because:

- Trainees do not have to go "on stage" and confront a large audience when they undertake the more demanding supervisory role.
- Trainees learn vicariously by being actively involved in each practice round: by playing the role of supervisor in one round, the role of subordinate in another, and by preparing to give feedback in the role of observer in one round (in a three-person group) or two rounds (in a four-person group).
- Feedback from fellow trainees provides greater credibility to the trainee playing supervisor than feedback solely from the trainer. And feedback from two trainee observers (in a four-person group) is more credible than from only one (in a three-person group).
- Small groups are easier for the instructor to observe and to provide corrective feedback to.

### *Needed Rolesets*

Four different roleplay situations will be needed for four-person groups, organized in rolesets like those presented in Appendix B of Part II. Three different roleplay situations will be needed for three-person groups, organized in rolesets like those presented in Appendix C of Part II. Each roleset contains exercise instructions, and the roles to be played or observed in each of four rounds (for four-person groups) or each of three rounds (for three-person groups).

Ideally, as for demonstration modeling, practice roleplays for the trainees should be based on input from experienced personnel as to challenging situations the trainees are likely to encounter, and ones that relate to the activity of the learning-point module to be demonstrated. Again, useful ideas can be solicited by means of a form like the *Roleplay Input Form* presented in Appendix A of Part II.

### *Mental Rehearsal*

After being assigned to groups, viewing and discussing the demonstration modeling as a group as a whole, the trainees will break into their practice groups to implement the roleplays (having been given their rolesets to study in advance). There is evidence that mental review of the learning points by the trainee playing "supervisor"—immediately before overt rehearsal—facilitates his or her ability to remember the learning points and properly reproduce the modeled behavior.[40]

In fact, there is evidence that mental practice, alone, produces some of the positive effects of overt practice. For example, McFall and Twentyman found that mental rehearsal significantly increased trainee assertiveness behavior, in comparison with, no-rehearsal controls.[41] Decker found that mental rehearsal significantly enhanced the generalization of assertiveness behavior to a novel situation,[42] and McFall and Lillesand found that overt-plus-mental-rehearsal, assertiveness trainees improved significantly more than overt-rehearsal-only trainees.[43] Finally, Feltz and Landers make the point that, generally, activities that rely more upon cognitive processing benefit more from mental rehearsal than those that involve simple motor acts.[44]

Interestingly, there are reports that mental rehearsal has something in common with the observation of modeling—that both produce alterations of muscular potentials that are similar in pattern to those produced by overt performance.[45]

### *Feedback*

Evidence shows that feedback (knowledge of how accurately and effectively one has implemented the learning points) is essential for efficient learning, and that, for greatest effectiveness, it should be timely, specific, and credible.[46] Therefore, immediately after a roleplay, it is useful to have the trainee playing the subordinate give his or her reactions: Did the "supervisor" provide ample opportunity to communicate her or his feelings and/or relevant information? Does he or she feel better or worse about the situation than when the interview started? Why?

Next, trainee observers, using their *Observer Forms* (see Appendix A of Part II), should indicate how accurately and completely the trainee playing the supervisor adhered to the learning points. And last, the "supervisor" should be invited to give her or his reactions to the roleplay. Typically, most of these responses will be positive, and this will further enhance trainee motivation to master successful implementation.

Though the repeated playing of a supervisory role is the most direct basis for learning to occur, it is not the only basis. Vicarious learning occurs when trainees act as roleplay subordinates and observers.

### *Use of Videotape Playback*

There have been mixed results as to the usefulness of immediate videotape playback of a trainee's first roleplays. This type of feedback is probably more important for motor-skill development (as for mastering a golf swing) than for cognitive-skill development. We need more information about the conditions under which it may be useful for the latter. Presently, instructors who plan to use it should wait until their trainees—especially the less-experienced ones—have become reasonably comfortable with roleplaying.[47]

## Follow-Up

The primary goal of supervisory training is *not* retention and implementation in the training environment, it is effective, new-skill transfer to various job situations over an extended period of time. Key motivators toward this end will be:

- the understanding and use (modeling) of the new skills by higher-level personnel (why they should be the first to be trained),
- periodic, anonymous feedback from subordinates as to the extent to which their supervisor are utilizing the new skills, and
- incorporation of this feedback into the determination of formal rewards and penalties for managers at all levels.

In addition, effective follow-up requires overlearning, on-the-job practice, and remedial action, as are discussed below.

### *The Need for Overlearning*

Frequently in supervisory skills training, there is the problem of proactive inhibition: the threat of old, well-established behaviors to the retention of new and different ones. Without deliberate "overlearning"—practice beyond that required for short-term mastery and retention—trainees will tend to revert to old behaviors when they experience stress.[48]

The problem is greatest when two competing systems of behavior are related to the same discriminative stimulus or antecedent cue. This is often the case with supervisory behavior, when we want to displace less productive ways of responding to given situations with more productive ones.[49] Interestingly, Saltz found that the disrupting potential of an old, established response *increases* when the new behavior is unused for an extended period of time.[50]

Overlearning is most productive when it is based on a variety of realistic and challenging roleplays that represent authentic situations that the trainees are likely to encounter. Such roleplays will enhance the credibility of the training, facilitate the transfer of skills learned to everyday work situations, and sustain a high level of trainee interest. The best source for such roleplays is to have trainees describe challenging individual performance-problem situations they have encountered personally. A useful tool for collecting such information is a form such as the *Roleplay Input Form* presented in Appendix A of Part II.

### *The Need For On-The-Job Practice and Remedial Action*

A large part of the trainee's practice for overlearning should be conducted on the job. Therefore, a follow-up phase of the training program should include assigned work-site implementation, with trainees reporting their experiences back to scheduled training-group follow-up sessions for discussion and any needed remedial action (see the discussion of homework assignments under Phase Three Activity in Part II).

As is discussed in Part II, if a particular trainee plans to seek assistance from the group, she or he should prepare a description of the unsuccessful interview situation in advance for distribution (using the *Roleplay Input Form*) so that the situation can be understood by the group and roleplayed before it. Typically, the submitting supervisor had failed to implement the learning points appropriately, but "showing" is more effective than "telling." Also, the credibility of the roleplay is enhanced when the submitting supervisor plays the role of the subordinate.

These follow-up sessions should be continued as long as the trainees feel a need for them, although, with an increasing time interval between meetings.

## Acceptability to Trainees

Behavior modeling has inherent "face validity" for trainees: it clearly relates to the kinds of problems they experience, observe, or hear about every day.

The learning points are grounded in sound theory, and they serve as practical, attainable, and motivating goals. When trainees experience the successful use of them, and watch others do the same, they are encouraged to experiment with them in their everyday behavior.

Successful trainee experience is almost assured by completion of a prepractice learning-points exercise that utilizes a worksheet like the *Learning Points Worksheet* in Appendix A of Part II (see the discussion of this in the Phase One Activity section of Part II). As a result, most trainees will effectively implement at least 70% of the learning points in their first roleplaying practice as "supervisors." Such good initial success will sustain and enhance interest in the training, as well as feelings of self-efficacy or confidence. It will also provide a solid basis for the instructor to build on: "Good going, Jack, with all of the learning points except the third. Let's see you include it next time."

As was documented above, we now know that optimal success with behavior modeling requires adequate implementation of all four components: use of appropriate learning points, demonstration modeling of the learning points, trainee practice with feedback, and follow-up remedial action and reinforcement.

## Background Overview of Applications

The effectiveness of behavior modeling as a training tool has been appreciated for centuries by instructors in various trades, sports, medicine, the theater, and martial arts, because the approach is intuitively appealing and demonstrably effective. Its venerability is illustrated by the film *Spartacus* which dramatizes its use for the training of Roman gladiators. This seems a likely representation, in view of the fact that the Romans established special schools for gladiators.[51]

Flexner tells us that Dr. Boerhaave used the approach at the University of Leyden in the early 1700s. He insisted that his medical students examine patients in his presence—after appropriate instruction-demonstration—and then receive feedback from him about their performance. However, he apparently saw no need to formally record the nature and importance of the approach for the benefit of other instructors.[52]

Flexner laments this failure to "pass the torch" in discussing the need for assured clinical instruction. He illustrates the prevailing lack of it with the case of Dr. Helmholtz, a military-surgeon graduate of 1842, who gave public lectures about operating on tumors, though he had never seen a tumor cut! In fact, until well after 1912, many other medical students were permitted to graduate without hands-on experience.

### First Written Presentation

The first written presentation of the basic components of behavior-modeling training the author has found is in a book on developing manual skills written by C. M. Woodward in 1887.[53] He stresses the essentiality of using learning points, demonstration modeling, and trainee rehearsal with feedback from fellow trainees, as well as from the instructor. And he describes how various centers of vocational training in the United States were preceded by earlier efforts; such as, the Free Institute founded in Worchester, Massachusetts in 1868; The Imperial Technical School of Moscow (where Victor Della-Vos introduced the Russian method of class instruction in the use of tools in 1868); the Artisans' School at Rotterdam established in 1869; the Apprentice School for the City of Paris, opened in 1873; and Finsbury College in London (founding date not given).

On the basis of Woodward's discussion, one can reasonably infer that at least two of these schools used behavior-modeling procedures in a planned and systematic way.

### Use of in World War I

A form of behavior modeling, the Bleriot System, was used to train World War I pilots at Avord, France.[54] Students learned to fly in single-seat machines, unaccompanied by an instructor. As they completed appropriate instruction and demonstration-guided practice, they progressed in easy stages—with few serious injuries—from nonflyable "penguins" (clipped-wing Bleriots), to flyable ones.

First, they taxied penguins, until they could make six straight runs at about 40 miles per hour. Then, they continued this type of practice in the "rouleur" (roller) class with regular Bleriots, just below flying speed (about thirty miles per hour). Next, they entered the "decollet" (take-off) class, in which they would go up only six to nine feet, and then settle down by reducing speed. Next, the "pique classes" (first and advanced stages) in which they flew higher, and practiced pointing the craft's nose toward the ground. Lastly, they completed a "petit voyage"—a cross-country flight.

The approach permitted relatively few instructors to effectively and safely handle large numbers of students. Yet, the author has yet to find any reference in the literature to a written manual, or operational reports, about this training.

We see formal presentation of the basic elements of behavior modeling again in 1919 by Charles Allen, who was given the job of designing a training program for U.S. shipyard instructors during World War I.[55] He taught more than 1,000 of them, while directing the instructor-training work of the Emergency Fleet Corporation. In turn, according to Mattox, the Emergency Fleet Corporation oversaw an increase in the number of U.S. shipyard workers from approximately 50,000 in 1917 to 301,627 by January 1919.[56]

Allen's basic steps are:

- determination of related skills and associated knowledge to be taught,
- preparation,
- presentation,
- application, and
- follow-up.

Among his observations:

> The teacher, therefore, is not the driver, but the skilled director of the learner's activity ... the man must be trained so that he can "pull together" his trade ability, his technical knowledge, and his trade experience to meet the demands of different trade situations ... this is the generalization phase of instruction.[57]

## Use of in World War II

Building on Allen's World War I work, Glen Gardiner and M. J. Kane developed the highly successful, behavior-modeling-based, Job-Instruction-Training (JIT) component of the Within Industry (TWI) program of World War II.

From August 1940 to September 1945, four national directors trained 22 regional directors. They, in turn, trained 200 TWI Institute conductors. Eventually, 23,000 trainers effectively trained some 1.75 million supervisors in 16,500 plants. Anecdotal accounts and testimonials about the program's accomplishments are impressive. Among the more specific ones:

> An Oregon shipbuilding company reported that JIT was responsible for increasing output from 800 to 3200 rivets per man, per day, per shift.
>
> All 600 plants that responded to a survey reported that JIT had significantly reduced training time required to get workers up to production, with 23 percent reporting reductions of 50 percent or more.
>
> The Curtis-Wright Aircraft Company reported a per capita scrap cost of 15 cents for a department in which all supervisors had received JIT certification, 27 cents for a comparable department in which 83 percent had received certification, and 65 cents for a comparable department in which only 25 percent had received certification.[58]

## Other Uses

There is a 1942 report of behavior modeling having been used for therapeutic purposes.[59] And following World War II, JIT was sponsored for many years by the private Training Within Industry Foundation,[60] with subsequent refinements to JIT procedures being reported by Gardner.[61] Then, the middle 1970s saw the first application of behavior modeling to supervisory skills training. Bell Telephone, General Electric, and IBM were among the first to conduct research about its effectiveness.[62]

## Notes

1. A. J. Falcone, J. E. Edwards, and R. R. Rice, "Meta analysis of Personnel Training Techniques for Three Populations." Paper presented at the annual Academy of Management Meetings, Chicago, 1986; Paul Taylor, "The Transferability of Behavior Modeling Training Across Organizations and Cultures," paper presented at the July, 1994 International HRM Conference in Queensland, Australia. Also, see "Behavior Modeling," a review of research by Darlene Russ-Eft in *What Works: Training and Development Practices*, Laurie J. Bassi and Darlene Russ-Eft (Eds.), American Society for Training and Development, 1997, pages 105-149.

2. In Mel Schnake, Editor, Southern Management Association 1992 Proceeding, pages 279-284. Published by the Southern Management Association.

3. S. Epstein, "The Stability of Behavior: On Predicting Most of the People Much of the Time," *Journal of Personality and Social Psychology*, Vol. 37, 1979, pages 1097-1126. Also see K. Bowers, "Situationalism in Psychology: An Analysis and a Critique," *Psychological Review*, Vol. 80, 1973, pages 307-336; N. Endler and D. Magnusson, "Toward an Interactional Psychology of Personality," *Psychology Bulletin*, Vol. 83, 1976, pages 956-974; and J. R. McNamara and C. A. Blumer, "Role Playing to Assess Social Competence: Ecological Validity Considerations," *Behavior Modification*, Vol. 6, 1982, pages 519-549.

4. A. J. Marrow, D. G. Bowers, and S. E. Seashore, *Management by Participation*. New York: Harper and Row, 1967, pages 56-59, 154, 202-213; R. Likert, *The Human Organization: Its Management and Value*. New York: McGraw Hill, 1967, page 80; J. C. Taylor and D. Bowers, *Survey of Organizations: Toward a Machine-Scored, Standardized Questionnaire Instrument*. Ann

Arbor: Institute for Social Research, University of Michigan, 1972, pages 89-102; J. L. Franklin, "Down the Organization: Influence Levels Across Levels of Hierarchy, *Administrative Science Quarterly*, Vol. 20, 1975, pages 153-164; R. Likert and J. G. Likert, *New Ways of Managing Conflict*. New York: McGraw-Hill, 1976, pages 71-86.

5. M. Sorcher and R. Spence, "The Interface Project: Behavior Modeling as Social Technology in South Africa," *Personnel Psychology*, Vol. 35, 1982, pages 557-581.

6. R. F. Burnaska, "The Effect of Behavior Modeling Training Upon Managers' Behavior and Employees' Perceptions," *Personnel Psychology*, Vol. 29, 1976, pages 329-335.

7. M. S. Viteles, *Industrial Psychology*. New York: W. W. Norton and Company, 1932.

8. T. L. Rosenthal, "Modeling Therapies." In M. Hersen, R. Eisler and P. Miller (Eds.), *Progress in Behavior Modification*, Volume 2. New York: Academic Press, 1976.

9. C. L. Hull, "Quantitative Aspects of the Evolution of Concepts, An Experimental Study," *Psychological Monographs*, Vol. 28 (whole No. 123), 1920.

10. A. Bandura, *Social Learning Theory*. Englewood Cliffs, NJ: Prentice-Hall, 1986.

11. A. Bandura, *Social Foundations of Thought and Action*. Englewood Cliffs, NJ: Prentice-Hall, 1986. Especially Chapter 2 on observational learning.

12. E. Saltz, *The Cognitive Bases of Human Learning*. Homewood, IL: The Dorsey Press, 1971.

13. E. Saltz, *The Cognitive Bases of Human Learning*. Homewood, IL: The Dorsey Press, 1971; M. R. Goldfried, "Toward the Delineation of Therapeutic Change Principles," *American Psychologist*, Vol 35, 1980, pages 991-999.

14. H. C. Triandis, "Incongruence Between Intentions and Behavior: A Review." Paper presented at the Symposium on Consistency of Attitudes, Intentions, and Behavior at the American Psychological Association Meetings, Washington, 1982.

15. A. Bandura, *Social Foundations of Thought and Action*. Englewood Cliffs, NJ: Prentice-Hall, 1986.

16. M. D. Spiegler, R. M. Liebert, M. McMains and L. E. Fernandez, "Experimental Development of a Modeling Treatment to Extinguish Persistent Avoidance Behavior." In R. Rubin and C. Franks (Eds.), *Advances in Behavior Therapy*. New York, Academic Press, 1969; P. H. Friedman, "The Effects of Modeling and Role-Playing on Assertive Behavior." In R. D. Rubin, et al. (Eds.), *Advances in Behavior Therapy*. New York: Academic Press, 1971; T. L. Rosenthal and W. R. Carroll, "Factors in Vicarious Modification of Complex Grammatical Parameters," *Journal of Educational Psychology*, Vol. 63, 1972, pages 174-178. A. Bandura and R. Jeffery, "Role of Symbolic Coding and Rehearsal Processes in Observational Learning," *Journal of Personality and Social Psychology*, Vol. 26, 1973, pages 122-130; A. P. Goldstein, J. Martens, H. Hubben, H. van Belle, W. Schaaf, H. Wiersma, and A. Goedhart, "The Use of Modeling to Increase Independent Behavior," *Behavior Research and Therapy*, Vol. 11, 1973, Experiment 3; P. J. Decker, "The Enhancement of Behavior Modeling Training of Supervisory Skills by the Inclusion of Retention Processes," *Personnel Psychology*, Vol. 32, 1982, pages 323-332; P. J. Decker, "Effects of Different Symbolic Coding Stimuli in Behavior Modeling Training," *Personnel Psychology*, Vol. 37, 1984, pages 711-720.

17. R. M. McFall and C. T. Twentyman, "Four Experiments in the Relative Contributions of Rehearsal, Modeling, and Coaching to Assertion Training," *Journal of Abnormal Psychology*, Vol. 81, 1973, Experiment 1; A. P. Goldstein and M. Sorcher, *Changing Supervisory Behavior*. New York: Pergamon Press. 1974. page 60; B. J. Zimmerman and T. Rosenthal, "Conserving and Retaining Equalities and Inequalities Through Observation and Correction," *Development Psychology*, Vol. 10, 1974; B. J. Zimmerman and T. Rosenthal, "Observational Learning of Rule-governed Behavior by Children," *Psychological Bulletin*, Vol. 81, 1974; P. J. Decker, "Effects of Different Symbolic Coding Stimuli in Behavior Modeling Training," *Personnel Psychology*, Vol. 37, 1984, pages 711-720.

18. G. P. Latham and L. M. Saari, "The Application of Social Learning Theory to Training Supervisors Through Behavior Modeling," *Journal of Applied Psychology*, Vol. 64, 1979, pages 239-246; E. A. Locke, K. N. Shaw, L. M. Saari and G. P. Latham, "Goal-setting and Task Performance: 1969-1980," *Psychological Bulletin*, Vol. 90, 1981, pages 125-152.

19. A. Bandura, *Social Learning Theory*. Englewood Cliffs, NJ: Prentice-Hall, 1977. Useful ideas for instruction to develop complex, problem-solving skills may be found in Jeroen J. G. van Merrienboer's *Training Complex Cognitive Skills: A Four-Component Instructional Design Model for Technical Training*. Englewood Cliffs, NJ: Educational Technology Publications, 1997.

20. J. C. Flanagan, "The Critical Incident Technique," *Psychosocial Bulletin*, Vol. 51, 1954, pages 327-358; G. Fivars, "The Critical Incident Technique: A Bibliography," *JAS Catalog of Selected Documents in Psychological*, Vol. 5, 1975.

21. G. A. Miller, "The Magical Number Seven, Plus or Minus Two: Some Limits on Our Capacity for Processing Information," *Psychological Review*, Vol. 63, 1956, pages 81-97.

22. P. J. Decker, "Effects of Symbolic Coding and Rehearsal in Behavior-modeling Training," *Journal of Applied Psychology*, Vol. 65, 1980, pages 625-634.

23. G. P. Latham and G. A. Yukl, "A Review of Research on the Application of Goal Setting in Organizations," *Academy of Management Journal*, Vol. 18, 1975, pages 824-845; E. A Locke, K. N. Shaw, L. M. Saari and G. P. Latham, "Goal- setting and Task Performance: 1969-1980," *Psychology Bulletin*, Vol. 90, 1981, pages 125-152.

24. For example, see M. E. Gist, C. Schwoerer, and B. Rosen, "Effects of Alternative Training Methods on Self-Efficacy and Performance in Computer Software Training," *Journal of Applied Psychology*, Vol. 74, 1989, pages 884-891.

25. R. D. O'Connor, "Modification of Social Withdrawal Through Symbolic Modeling," *Journal of Applied Behavior Analysis*, Vol. 2, 1969, pages 15-22; R. D. O'Connor, "Relative Efficacy of Modeling, Shaping, and the Combined Procedures for Modification of Social Withdrawal," *Journal of Abnormal Psychology*, Vol. 79, 1972, pages 327-334.

26. P. H. Friedman, "The Effects of Modeling and Role-playing on Assertive Behavior." In R. D. Rubin, et al. (Eds.), *Advances in Behavior Therapy*. New York: Academic Press, 1971; E. Young, D. Rim, and T. Kennedy, "An Experimental Investigation of Modeling and Verbal Reinforcement in the Modification of Assertive Behavior," *Behavior Research and Therapy*, Vol. 11, 1973, pages 317-319; R. M. McFall and J. R. Galbraith, "Two Studies Examining Feedback in Assertion Training," 1977. Reported by C. T. Twentyman and R. T. Zimmerman in "Behavioral Training of Social Skills: A Critical Review." In M. Hersen, R. M. Eisler and P. M. Miller (Eds.), *Progress in Behavior Modification*, Volume 7. New York: Academic Press, 1979.

27. A. P. Goldstein, J. Martens, H. Hubben, H. van Belle, W. Schaaf, H. Wiersma and A. Goedhart, "The Use of Modeling to Increase Independent Behavior," *Behavior Research and Therapy*, Vol. 11, 1973, (three experiments).

28. G. L. Stone and A. Vance, "Instructions, Modeling, and Rehearsal: Implications for Training," *Journal of Counseling Psychology*, Vol. 23, 1976, pages 272-279.

29. T. L. Rosenthal, "Modeling Therapies." In M. Hersen, R. Eisler and P. Miller (Eds.), *Progress in Behavior Modification*, Volume 2. New York: Academic Press, 1976.

30. David Shapiro and Diana Shapiro, "Meta-analysis of Comparative Therapy Outcome Studies: A Replication and Refinement," *Psychological Bulletin*, Vol. 92, 1982, pages 581-604.

31. For examples, see P. H. Friedman, "The Effects of Modeling and Role-playing on Assertive Behavior." In R. D. Rubin, et al. (Eds.), *Advances in Behavior Therapy*. New York: Academic Press, 1971; R. M. McFall and C. T. Twentyman, "Four Experiments in the Relative Contributions of Rehearsal, Modeling, and Coaching to Assertion Training," *Journal of Abnormal Psychology*, Vol. 81, 1973, pages 199- 218; J. Curran, "An Evaluation of a Skills Training Program and a Systematic Desensitization Program in Reducing Dating Anxiety," *Behavior Research and Therapy*, Vol. 13, 1975, pages 65-68; J. Curran and F. Gilbert, "A Test of the Relative Effectiveness of a Systematic Desensitization Program and a Interpersonal Skills Training Program With Date Anxious Subjects," *Behavior Therapy*, Vol. 6, 1975, pages 510-521; J. C. Wright, "A Comparison of Systematic Desensitization Modification of Social Fear," *Behavior Therapy*, Vol. 7, 1976, pages 205-210.

32. A. Bandura, D. Ross and S. Ross, "A Comparative Test of the Status Envy, Social Power, and Secondary Reinforcement Theories of Identifactory Learning," *Journal of Abnormal and Social Psychological*, Vol. 67, 1963, pages 527-534; A. Bandura and C. Kupers, "Transmission of Patterns of Self-reinforcement Through Modeling," *Journal of Abnormal and Social Psychological*, Vol. 69, 1964, pages 1-9; A. P. Goldstein, J. Martens, H. Hubben, H. van Belle, W. Schaaf, H. Wiersma and A. Goedhart, "The Use of Modeling to Increase Independent Behavior," *Behavior Research and Therapy*, Vol. 11, 1973, Experiment 2; A. P. Goldstein and M. Sorcher, *Changing Supervisory Behavior*. New York: Pergamon Press, 1974; K. Bussey and D. Perry, "Sharing Reinforcement Contingencies With a Model: A Social-learning Analysis of Similarity Effects in Imitation Research," *Journal of Personality and Social Psychology*, Vol. 34, 1976, pages 1168-1176; D. Gould and M. Weiss, "Effect of Model Similarity and Model Self-talk on Self-efficacy in Muscular Endurance," *Journal of Sport Psychology*, Vol. 3, 1981, pages 17-29.

33. A. P. Goldstein and M. Sorcher, *Changing Supervisory Behavior*. New York: Pergamon Press, 1974; A. Bandura, *Social Foundations of Thought and Action*. Englewood Cliffs, NJ: Prentice-Hall, 1986.

34. J. Mann, "Vicarious Desensitization of Test Anxiety Through Observation of Videotaped Treatment," *Journal of Counseling Psychology*, Vol. 19, 1972, pages 1-7; D. L. Feltz, D. Landers and J. Raeder, "Enhancing Self-efficacy in High-avoidance Motor Tasks: A Comparison of Modeling Techniques," *Journal of Social Psychology*, Vol. 1, 1979, pages 112-122; A. Bandura, *Social Foundations of Thought and Action*. Englewood Cliffs, NJ: Prentice-Hall, 1986, many studies cited.

35. C. P. Duncan, "Transfer After Training With Single Versus Multiple Tasks," *Journal of Experimental Psychology*, Vol. 55, 1958, pages 63-72; H. C. Ellis, *The Transfer of Learning*. New York: Macmillan, 1965.

36. A. Bandura and F. Menlove, "Factors Determining Vicarious Extinction Avoidance Behavior Through Symbolic Modeling," *Journal of Personality and Social Psychology*, Vol. 8, 1968, pages 99-108; A. Kazdin, "Comparative Effects of Some Variations of Covert Modeling," *Journal of Behavior Therapy and Experimental Psychiatry*, Vol. 5, 1974, pages 225-232; A. Kazdin, "Effects of Covert Modeling, Multiple Models, and Model Reinforcement on Assertive Behavior," *Behavior Therapy*, Vol. 7, 1976, pages 211-222.

37. E. Shore and L. Sechrest, "Concept Attainment as a Function of Positive Instances Presented," *Journal of Educational Psychology*, Vol. 52, 1961, pages 303-307.

38. L. E. Bourne and D. Guy, "Learning Conceptual Rules: The Role of Positive and Negative Instances," *Journal of Experimental Psychology*, Vol. 77, 1968, pages 488-494; L. E. Bourne, "Knowing and Using Concepts," *Psychological Review*, Vol. 77, 1970, pages 546-556; F. Craik and R. Lockhart, "Levels of Processing: A Framework for Memory Research," *Journal of Verbal Learning and Verbal Behavior*, Vol. 11, 1972, pages 671-684.

39. A. Bandura, "Influence of Models' Reinforcement Contingencies on the Acquisition of Imitative Responses," *Journal of Personality and Social Psychology*, Vol. 1, 1965, pages 589-595; P. H. Friedman, "The Effects of Modeling and Role-playing on Assertive Behavior. In R. D. Rubin, et al. (Eds.), *Advances in Behavior Therapy*. New York: Academic Press, 1971, pages 149-169; A. P. Goldstein and M. Sorcher, *Changing Supervisory Behavior*. New York: Pergamon Press, 1974; G. Salvendy and J. Piltsis, "The Development and Validation of an Analytical Training Program for Medical Suturing," *Human Factors*, Vol. 22, 1980, pages 753-770.

40. D. Michael and N. Maccoby, "Factors Influencing the Effects of Student Participation on Verbal Learning From Films: Motivating Versus Practice Effects, 'Feedback,' and Overt Versus Covert Responding." In A. A. Lumsdaine (Ed.), *Student Response in Programmed Instruction*. Washington, DC: National Academy of Sciences-National Research Council, 1961; E. Ulich, "Some Experiments on the Function of Mental Training in the Acquisition of Motor Skills," *Ergonomics*, Vol. 10, 1967, pages 411-419; E. Rawlings, I. Rawlings, S. Chen, and D. Yilk, "The Facilitating of Mental Rehearsal in the Acquisition of Rotary Pursuit Tracking," *Psychonomic Science*, Vol. 26, 1972, Experiment 2; A. Bandura and R. Jeffery, "Role of Symbolic Coding and Rehearsal Processes in Observational Learning," *Journal of Personality and Social Psychology*, Vol. 26, 1973, pages 122-130; R. W. Jeffrey, "The Influence of Symbolic and Motor Rehearsal in Observational Learning," *Journal of Research in Personality*, Vol. 10, 1976, pages 116-127; J. M. Silva, "Competitive Sport Environments: Performance Enhancement Through Cognitive Intervention," *Behavior Modification*, Vol. 6, 1982, pages 443-463.

41. R. M. McFall and C. T. Twentyman, "Four Experiments in the Relative Contributions of Rehearsal, Modeling, and Coaching to Assertion Training," *Journal of Abnormal Psychology*, Vol. 81, 1973, pages 199-218.

42. P. J. Decker, "Effects of Symbolic Coding and Rehearsal in Behavior-modeling training," *Journal of Applied Psychology*, Vol. 65, 1980, pages 625-634.

43. R. M. McFall and D. Lillesand, "Behavior Rehearsal With Modeling and Coaching in Assertion Training," *Journal of Abnormal Psychology*, Vol. 77, 1971, pages 313-323.

44. D. L. Feltz and D. Landers, "Effects of Mental Practice on Motor Skill Learning and Performance: A Meta-analysis," *Journal of Social Psychology*, Vol. 5, 1983, pages 25-57. Also, see J. E. Driskell, C. Cooper and A. Moran, "Does Mental Practice Enhance Performance?," *Journal of Applied Psychology*, Vo1. 79, 1994, pages 481-492, and "Survival of the Busiest," an excerpt in *The Wall Street Journal*, October 11, 2002, pages B1 and B4, from a forthcoming book, *The Mind and Brain: Neuroplasticity and the Power of Mental Force*, by Jeffrey Schwartz and Sharon Begley (to be published by Regan Books), about how parts of the brain expand and rewire through use.

45. E. Ulich, "Some Experiments on the Function of Mental Training in the Acquisition of Motor Skills," *Ergonomics*, Vol. 10, 1967, pages 411-419; J. M. Silva, "Competitive Sport Environments: Performance Enhancement Through Cognitive Intervention," *Behavior Modification*, Vol. 6, 1982, pages 443-463.

46. D. Michael and N. Maccoby, "Factors Influencing the Effects of Student Participation on Verbal Learning From Films: Motivating Versus Practice Effects, 'Feedback,' and Overt Versus Covert Responding." In A. A. Lumsdaine (Ed.), *Student Response in Programmed Instruction*. Washington, DC: National Academy of Sciences-National Research Council, 1961; K. N. Wexley and C. Thornton, "Effect of Verbal Feedback of Test Results Upon Learning," *Journal of Educational Research*, Vol. 66, 1972, pages 119-121.

47. J. Melnick, "A Comparison of Replication Techniques in the Modification of Minimal Dating Behavior," *Journal of Abnormal Psychology*, Vol. 81, 1973, pages 51-59; I. G. Sarason and V. Ganzer, "Modeling and

Group Discussion in the Rehabilitation of Juvenile Delinquents," *Journal of Counseling Psychology*, Vol. 20, 1973, pages 442-449; M. F. Prout, "An Analogue Study Assessing the Effects of Three Training Procedures on Non-verbal Assertive Behavior." Reviewed in M. Hersen, R. M. Eisler and P. M. Miller (Eds.), *Progress in Behavior Modification*, Volume 7. New York: Academic Press, 1979, pages 319-400; J. Gormally, C. Hill, M. Otis, and L. Rainey, "A Microtraining Approach to Assertion Training," *Journal of Counseling Psychology*, Vol. 22, 1975, pages 299-303; J. Melnick and R. Stocker, "An Experimental Analysis of the Behavioral Rehearsal With Feedback Technique in Assertiveness Training," *Behavior Therapy*, Vol. 8, 1977, pages 222-228; R. M. McFall and J. Galbraith, "Two Studies Examining Feedback in Assertion Training, Unpublished manuscript, University of Wisconsin, 1977. Reviewed in M. Hersen, R. M. Eisler and P. M. Miller (Eds.), *Progress in Behavior Modification*, Volume 7. New York: Academic Press, 1979, pages 319-400.

48. E. Saltz, *The Cognitive Bases of Human Learning*. Homewood, IL: The Dorsey Press, 1971, pages 197, 206; A. P. Goldstein and M. Sorcher, *Changing Supervisory Behavior.* New York: Pergamon Press, 1974, pages 61-62, 75.

49. E. Saltz, *The Cognitive Bases of Human Learning*. Homewood, IL: The Dorsey Press, 1971, pages 197-206.

50. Ibid.; J. D. Schendel and J. Hagman, "On Sustaining Procedural Skills Over A Prolonged Retention Interval," *Journal of Applied Psychology*, Vol. 67, 1982, pages 605-610; J. E. Driskell, R. P. Willis, and C. Cooper, "Effect of Overlearning on Retention," *Journal of Applied Psychology*, Vol. 77, 1992, pages 615-692.

51. See M. Grant, *Gladiators*. London: Weidenfeld and Nicolson, 1967, pages 39-40, 49-50.

52. A. Flexner, *Medical Education in Europe*. Carnegie Foundation for the Advancement of Teaching: Bulletin No. 6, 1912, pages 4-5.

53. The Manual Training School. Boston: D. C. Heath and Company.

54. See C. Nordhoff and J. Hall, *Falcons of France*. New York: Little Brown, 1929, Chapters 2 and 3. Both men completed this training.

55. Charles R. Allen, *The Instructor, the Man and the Job.* Philadelphia: J. B. Lipincott Company, 1919.

56. W. C. Mattox, *Building the Emergency Fleet*. Cleveland: The Penton Publishing Company, 1920, page 70.

57. Allen, Op. cit., pages 129-131.

58. *The Training Within Industry Report 1940-1945.* Washington: U.S. Printing Office, September 1945, especially Chapter 7.

59. G. E. Chittenden, "An Experimental Study in Measuring and Modifying Assertive Behavior in Young Children," *Monographs of the Society for Research in Child Development*, Vol. 7, No. 31, 1942.

60. W. D. Dietz, "On the Job Training and Training Within Industry Program." In Carl Heyel (Ed.), *The Encyclopedia of Management*. New York: Van Nostrand Reinhold Company, 1982, pages 770-772, 1247-1249.

61. J. E. Gardner, *Training Interventions in Job-skill Development*. Reading, MA: Addison-Wesley Publishing Company, 1981, especially pages 2-29.

62. A. P. Goldstein and M. Sorcher, *Changing Supervisory Behavior.* New York: Pergamon Press, 1974; A. I. Kraut, "Developing Managerial Skills Via Modeling Techniques: Some Positive Research Findings—A Symposium," *Personnel Psychology*, Vol. 29, 1976, pages 325-328.

## APPENDIX: EXAMPLES OF LEARNING-POINT MODULES

The first two modules below are most useful for dealing with a performance-related problem.

### NONJUDGMENTAL INFORMATION GATHERING

This module should be used before the *Remedial Action* module, and only one problem should be dealt with at a time.

- Explain, specifically, what you are concerned about and why you feel it is a problem, presenting any objective evidence you have, while withholding judgment of the person.
- Listen nonjudgmentally—to give person full opportunity to explain events and/or feelings—and encourage responding with comments, such as: "I see," "Can you tell me more about such and such?" and "What happened then?"
- When there is much input, "mirror back" what you have heard to check your understanding—for example: "as I understand it, you did this because …" or "you feel you have been unfairly accused because …"
- When needed, set a specific date for a follow-up meeting to permit you to collect information from other sources and/or to prepare for the next module, *Remedial Action.*

* * *

## Remedial Action

This module should be preceded by *Nonjudgmental Information Gathering* and only one problem at a time should be dealt with.

- State any solution requirements person may not be aware of.
- If simple resolution is not apparent, solicit and record person's ideas for solving the problem (on a blackboard or flipchart where both of you can see them)—giving no evaluation on your part at this time.
- Add your ideas—without evaluating them—then add any additional ideas that occur to either of you.
- Discuss and evaluate the ideas in terms of "pros" and "cons" associated with each (including the option of "no action").
- Seek agreement on a solution and spell out the specific steps to be taken by either, or both, of you. If you cannot agree and you have supervisory authority over the person, specify the action you will require, your reasons for requiring it, and when you expect it to occur (then skip the next step)
- When there is much input, "mirror back" what other is committed to. Agree on specific, follow-up meeting or observational time and date for reviewing progress or results.
- Praise the person as soon as feasible after successful implementation occurs (or for completion of a first step in a series of steps).

* * *

The following module is based on *Behavior Modeling Training* by Philip Decker and Barry Nathan, Praeger, 1985.

## When Person Fails to Properly Implement a Remedial Action Plan

- Define the problem in terms of lack of progress in properly implementing the steps agreed to earlier.
- Ask for, then nonjudgmentally listen to, reasons for the failure.
- If the reasons are not acceptable to you, explain why, and indicate any penalty that will be imposed now (if it was reasonable to expect the person to be aware of such a consequence prior to his or her failure) and/or any that will be imposed for continuing noncompliance
- If the original action plan is no longer appropriate, agree on needed changes and set a specific, follow-up meeting or observational time and date for reviewing progress or results.
- Express your confidence that the person can successfully achieve the new goal or goals.

* * *

The following Learning-Point Sets: Giving Recognition, Handling A Complaining Employee, Delegating Work, Handling Insubordination, Reducing Absenteeism, and Improving Safety Habits. are based on the *Supervisory Relationships Training Booklet* of AT&T.

## Giving Recognition

- Describe, specifically, what person did to deserve recognition and express your personal appreciation.
- Indicate your desire to know how you can be of assistance with any job-related problems or needs.
- If applicable, set the time and date for a specific follow-up meeting to see if concerns have been resolved.

* * *

## Handling a Complaining Employee

- Encourage full description of the complaint, by listening nonjudgmentally, without hostility or defensiveness—when needed, solicit additional information with queries, such as: "Can you tell me more about such and such ..." or "What happened then?"
- Communicate that you understand the person's viewpoint and feelings, and if the complaint is lengthy, do this by "mirroring back" what the person has said
- If you need to check with others and/or obtain additional information—or check to see if remedial action required by others has occurred—set a particular time and date for a follow-up meeting.
- If applicable, explain what corrective action you will take—or, if you cannot accommodate the person, nondefensively explain why.

* * *

## Delegating Work

- Put the person at ease and explain the purpose of the discussion.
- Clearly explain the work to be done and the requirements that the completed work must satisfy.
- Solicit comments and questions, and fully discuss these to achieve full understanding as to what will be done and a time and date for completion.
- Express appreciation for the person undertaking the assignment and confidence in the person's ability to complete it.

* * *

## Handling Insubordination

- If necessary, calm the person—take her/him to a private place.
- Fully explain the reasons for the instructions or order that was given.
- Ask for—and nonjudgmentally listen to—reasons for the failure to comply.
- If the explanation is not acceptable, explain the seriousness and possible consequences of his or her noncompliance.
- Give the person opportunity to reconsider.
- Express appreciation for compliance, or take appropriate disciplinary action.

* * *

## Reducing Absenteeism

- Withholding judgment, and in private, request reasons for absenteeism.
- Communicate that you understand employee's reasons and/or feelings.
- Explain relevant rules and how the absenteeism impacts on you and/or your group.
- Agree on steps to be taken for resolving problem causing the absenteeism (see remedial action module presented above).
- Follow-up for further action, or to commend for good attendance.

* * *

## Improving Safety Habits

- Describe, specifically, what you have seen, and why it concerns you.
- Describe the correct procedure and the reasons for it.
- Demonstrate the correct procedure, step by step.
- Observe employee trying it—provide approval or corrective feedback.
- Ask for ideas about how to maintain use of the correct procedure.
- Follow-up to correct, or to commend for correct performance.

* * *

## Conducting A Performance-Review Interview

- Explain that you have prepared in writing your tentative ratings on the merit factors, along with recorded, supporting, observed behaviors.
- Before sharing this information, invite the person to give his/her assessment on each factor with supporting reasons. (In light of the information provided, you may wish to revise your ratings immediately or set the time and date for a follow-up session to provide you with the opportunity to confirm or further process the new information).
- At the present meeting (or a later meeting) present your final appraisal, giving specific evidence for each rating.
- Solicit and discuss the person's comments or questions.
- When person's performance needs improvement, discuss and agree upon specific steps to be taken by the person (and you, if applicable), along with specific target dates.
- Commend the person for anything that was done well and express your willingness to assist, when requested, with development activity and goal achievement.

* * *

## Mediating Between Conflicting Individuals

- Get written commitment as to each party's willingness to search for resolution of the interpersonal problem, and refrain from sharing data generated with nonparticipants (assuring both parties in writing that this will be the case).
- Solicit written input from each party as to:
  - What the problem is.
  - What specific things the other party needs to:
    - start doing;

  - stop doing; and
  - do differently (explaining how in terms of overt, observable behaviors).
- Give this written input from each to the other party, soliciting a written response to:
  - Things I am willing to do (just needed to learn of need)—indicating what, where, and when (if answers are not obvious).
  - Things I would like to do, but will need help with (specifying help needed).
  - Things I feel are beyond my control to change (giving reasons).
  - Things I am unwilling to change (giving reasons).
- If further resolution is needed—in a meeting with both parties (on "neutral ground"), display on flipchart pages:
  - What each is willing to do (indicating what, when, and where, if answers are not obvious).
  - What each would like to do, provided specified help is given.
  - What each claims to have no control over.
  - What each is unwilling to change, with reasons given
- Where applicable, indicate what you are willing to do, or provide, to resolve the problem.

## Short Form for Supervisors to Use With Two Subordinates During a Meeting of the Three

- Ask each to state the problem as he/she sees it.
- Ask each to restate what the other has just said, soliciting confirmation or correction from the listener.
- Seek agreement on job-relevant/organization-relevant facts: problems, mutual needs, and/or goals (getting the disputants to like each other is not a goal)
- Ask for solutions and display these along with any you feel it necessary to include, on a flipchart or blackboard. Provide opportunity for each to discuss the pros and cons of the items, and to propose changes to them. Seek agreement on a solution.
- Set a specific follow-up meeting date to check progress.

If neither procedure above resolves the matter and you have supervisory authority over the persons involved, indicate what action you will require—giving your reasons—and indicate what penalty will be imposed for failure to comply

* * *

## Basic Learning Points for Many One-on-One Modules

- Focus on a specific behavior or problem—not the person.
- Encourage the person's full expression of ideas/feelings by listening nonjudgmentally.
- Seek agreement on a solution that makes clear the specific steps to be taken by either of you, with a specified target time and date for completion.
- Where applicable, agree on a specific meeting or observation time and date for reviewing progress or results.
- Maintain the person's self-esteem by:
  - Holding sessions in private.
  - Having your secretary hold nonemergency calls.
  - Rising when the person enters your office—going out from behind your desk to sit with him/her.
  - At end of session, stressing what is positive about the person's work and, where applicable, expressing confidence in her/his ability to implement what needs to be done.

# Part II

# Conduct of the Training

Part I provided a general overview of the nature of, and background to, behavior modeling, and significant evidence as to its effectiveness. Part II presents proven, detailed instructions for implementing the approach via use of the the two learning-point modules, *Nonjudgmental Information Gathering* and *Remedial Action*, for dealing with a subordinate-related problem.

## Preparing for the First Practice Session

### Selecting the First Trainees

The same learning points and training procedures apply, regardless of a trainee's rank, though the role-play situations selected should vary to provide greater credibility to the trainees. If you have a choice about whom to train first, start at the highest level possible, for higher-level managers usually exert the most influence on the behavior of subordinate managers. They signal what really matters—what will be rewarded and penalized—and they do this more through their actions than their pronouncements. In effect, they model behavior—for good or bad—for organizational members every working day. When they are the first to receive the training, they can more readily be positive models and recognize and commend the new behaviors on the part of their newly trained subordinates.

However, if their lack of understanding and support for the new behaviors creates a nonsupportive organizational climate, the chances for sustaining new behaviors on the job are greatly reduced.[1] In this event, even more attention must be given to the follow-up and transfer activities that are discussed later in Part II.

### Assigning the Trainees to Groups

Assign each trainee to a three-person or, preferably, four-person group, and record this information on a flipchart or blackboard for display at the first practice session. When necessary, groups of both three and four may be formed for the same practice session; however, this will mean that the four-person groups will not finish role-playing practice at the same time as the three-person groups, and different rolesets will be needed (see those in Appendix B compared with those in Appendix C). Use Table 1 to determine the combinations of three-person and four-person groups to form.

To facilitate concentration on learning, and to encourage trainees to play their parts realistically, avoid placing a subordinate with his or her supervisor, or good friends, in the same practice group.

### Needed Resources

- A live, modeling demonstration or, preferably, a demonstration videotape (based on the *Nonjudgmental Information Gathering* and *Remedial Action* learning-point modules) for dealing with a performance-related problem. If the trainees are from the same organization, the videotape should be made in-house, for the reasons discussed in Part I, with due regard to the various guidelines presented there.

**Table 1**

| *Number of Trainees* | *Number of Three Person Groups* | *Number of Four Person Groups* |
|---|---|---|
| 7 | 1 | 1 |
| 8 | 0 | 2 |
| 9 | 3 | 0 |
| 10 | 2 | 1 |
| 11 | 1 | 2 |
| 12 | 0 | 3 |
| 13 | 3 | 1 |
| 14 | 2 | 2 |
| 15 | 1 | 3 |
| 16 | 0 | 4 |
| 17 | 3 | 2 |
| 18 | 2 | 3 |
| 19 | 1 | 4 |
| 20 | 0 | 5 |
| 21 | 3 | 3 |
| 22 | 2 | 4 |
| 23 | 1 | 5 |
| 24 | 0 | 6 |
| 25 | 3 | 4 |
| 26 | 2 | 5 |
| 27 | 1 | 6 |
| 28 | 0 | 7 |
| 29 | 3 | 5 |
| 30 | 2 | 6 |
| 31 | 1 | 7 |
| 32 | 0 | 8 |
| 33 | 3 | 6 |
| 34 | 2 | 7 |
| 35 | 1 | 8 |
| 36 | 0 | 9 |
| 37 | 3 | 7 |
| 38 | 2 | 8 |
| 39 | 1 | 9 |
| 40 | 0 | 10 |

*Note:* To facilitate concentration on learning, and to encourage trainees to play their parts realistically, avoid placing a subordinate with his or her supervisor, or good friends, in the same practice group.

*Desirable:* A copy of the performance-problem, demonstration videotape, with the learning points presented (and/or narrated) with the scenes in which they are implemented—to be shown after discussion of the first-version showing.

- A roleset for each trainee, organized like the ones in Appendix B (for four-person groups) and Appendix C (for three-person groups). Ideally, these should be developed in-house when all trainees are associated with the same organization. Otherwise, the ones presented in Appendixes B and C are quite serviceable. Though they are relatively brief and of limited complexity, their use will facilitate trainees becoming accustomed to using the learning points in a roleplay setting. They have been used by the author with many groups, and have proven to be credible and productive. They also provide important guidance for the development of in-house material.

Four rolesets (for group members "W," "X," "Y," and "Z") are required for each four-person group, and these are presented in Appendix B. *You will need to make as many copies as needed of these (or of ones you have created in-house).* The four roleplays (designated below as A, B, C, and D) presented in these rolesets are played as follows (Sup. = Supervisor's Role, Sub. = Subordinate's Role):

| | Role-play | *Group Members* W | X | Y | Z |
|---|---|---|---|---|---|
| Round 1: | A | Sup. A (Robin Smith) | Observer | Sub. A (Carol Young) | Observer |
| Round 2: | B | Observer | Sup. B (Jerry Brown) | Observer | Sub B. (Chris Neely) |
| Round 3: | C | Sub. C (Jo James) | Observer | Sup. C (Lane Thomas) | Observer |
| Round 4: | D | Observer | Sub. D (Sandy Betts) | Observer | Sup. D (Rollin Jones) |

Since the roles that group members observe are presented in the roleplay sets, you can regroup for a "no-show" in a four-person group in the following manner:

- Should W not show up: Have X, Y, and Z play Rounds 2, 3, and 4. Have X or Z play Subordinate C in Round 3.
- Should X not show up: Have W, Y, and Z play Rounds 1, 3, and 4. Have W or Y play Subordinate D in Round 4.
- Should Y not show up: Have W, X, and Z play Rounds 1, 2, and 4. Have X or Z play Subordinate A in Round 1.
- Should Z not show up: Have W, X, and Y play Rounds 1, 2, and 3. Have W or Y play Subordinate B in Round 2.

Three rolesets (for group members "T," "U," and "V") are required for each three-person group, and these are presented in Appendix C. *You will need to make as many copies as needed of these (or of ones you have created in-house).* The three roleplays (designated below as A, B, and C) presented in these rolesets are played as follows (Sup. = Supervisor's Role, Sub. = Subordinate's Role):

| | *Roleplay* | *Group Members* T | U | V |
|---|---|---|---|---|
| Round 1: | A | Sup. A (Robin Smith) | Observer | Sub. A (Carol Young) |
| Round 2: | B | Sub. B (Chris Neely) | Sup. B (Jerry Brown) | Observer |
| Round 3: | C | Observer | Sub. C (Jo James) | Sup. C (Lane Thomas) |

- A trainee manual by the author for each trainee (available from Information Age Publishing).
- A meeting room with video playback equipment (if a modeling-demonstration videotape is available), and places for trainees to sit and write as they watch the live or taped demonstration.

  Subsequently, for role-playing practice, each group of three or four should be accommodated with a desk or table with two chairs (for the "supervisor" and "subordinate"), and one or two, armrest-desk chairs, so that the Observer (or two Observers in four-person groups) can write on the *Observer Form* during each roleplay.

  Whether or not these practice groups can be placed in one room depends upon the number of groups relative to the size of the room. Considerable interference can occur if groups are not at least 30 feet apart. If separate rooms are needed, they should be close enough to each other to provide ready access for you (or any needed assistants) to visit and observe each group during the practice period.
- Adequate time allowance for the first practice session. Generally, assuming that trainees will have studied their roles and associated materials for each round prior to the practice meeting, those acting as Observers should be instructed to allow a maximum of *8 minutes* for the role-play of each round and a maximum of *8 minutes* for the giving of feedback by two Observers. Consequently, you should allow *64 minutes* for the four rounds of practice in four-person groups. Three-person-group trainees who finish early can sit in as non-feedback-giving observers of four-person groups that have not finished.

  A typical two and one-third to two and three-fourths hours session will break down in the following manner:

| | |
|---|---|
| 30-45 minutes | *Phase One Activity:*<br>• Instructor discusses the *Nonjudgmental Information Gathering* and *Remedial Action* learning points,<br>• trainees view a live, performance-problem, modeling demonstration or, preferably, a performance-problem videotape, as they record on a *Learning Points Worksheet* each time that a learning point is implemented in the demonstration roleplay. |
| 64 minutes | *Phase Two Activity:*<br>Allow time for four practice rounds for four-person groups. |
| 45-60 minutes | *Phase Three Activity:*<br>• Instructor's observations (optional),<br>• Instructor fields questions, leads general discussion,<br>• Instructs trainees to use the learning points on the job, and then complete the *Homework Assignment Sheet* in the Appendix of the trainee manual,<br>• Sets the date for a follow-up meeting,<br>• Has trainees complete the End-of-Practice-Session Questionnaire (from the Appendix of trainee manual). |

Caution: Do not plan to videotape trainees in their first encounter with behavior-modeling practice. Good results will be obtained without doing this, and you will avoid the risk of arousing apprehensions that interfere with effective roleplaying and learning.

### Prepractice Activity

Assemble the trainees and:

- Distribute a W, X, Y, or Z roleset (from Appendix B or made in-house) to each trainee in a four-person group and distribute a T, U, or V roleset (from Appendix C or made in-house) to each trainee in a three-person group.

  Instruct the trainees to:
  - read the exercise instructions presented on the first page of their rolesets,
  - study the role of the Supervisor and the role of the Subordinate that each will play,
  - avoid looking at each other's rolesets until after the practice session, in order to enhance the realism of the roleplays and gain more benefit from the practice experience.

- Distribute a copy of the trainee manual to each trainee.

  Instruct the trainees to:

  - pay particular attention to the discussion *of the Nonjudgmental Information Gathering* and *Remedial Action* learning points, and to think about how they will use them in their roleplay, interview with a subordinate about his or her performance problem,
  - study the instructions at the beginning and end of the *Observer Form*, so that they can properly perform the duties of an Observer,
  - take the *Trainee Manual*, as well as a watch, to the practice session.

## The First Practice Session

### Phase One Activity

All trainees assemble in one room. Each has a writing surface for filling out the forms discussed below.

#### *Lead Discussion of the Learning Points*

Instructor: "From your review of the *Nonjudgmental Information Gathering* and the *Remedial Action* learning points in your manual, do you have any questions about what any of them mean, or how you would use them?"

If needed, the instructor should accept any proposed revisions in wording that do not alter basic meaning and are acceptable to all in the group.

Then, she or he should offer clarification in response to any questions about usage. (Note: The following notes about the learning points also appear in the *Trainee Manual*.)

## Discussion of the Nonjudgmental Information Gathering Learning Points

Note: This module should be used before the *Remedial Action* module, and only one problem should be dealt with at a time, so that the interviewer can remain better focused and have a better chance of achieving constructive closure.)

• **Explain, specifically, what you are concerned about and why you feel it is a problem, presenting any objective evidence you have, while withholding judgment of the person.**

Too often, we go off "half-cocked" with what turns out to be incomplete information and/or misperceptions—we assume that we *know* which problems exist and just what they are. The best protection against this danger is to present our perceptions as objectively as possible with the idea of encouraging the other person to give as full a response as he or she wishes to.

The other person will not feel as free to respond, or to do so in as constructive a manner, if he or she perceives us to be making an unwarranted accusation, or to be showing in our tone or manner that we have already determined the extent of "guilt" before a fair hearing.

True, you can unfairly chew someone out, and then apologize later when you discover that you were wrong, but why do needless damage, and jeopardize a relationship, when you don't have to?

• **Listen nonjudgmentally—to give person full opportunity to explain events and/or feelings—and encourage responding with comments, such as: "I see," "Can you tell me more about such and such?" and "What happened then?"**

It is not enough to *start off* objectively and nonjudgmentally, you must *stay this way* until the person has given as full a response as he or she wishes to. Premature arguments, contradictions, and judgments can "turn off" constructive responding in a hurry.

Being nonjudgmental does not signify agreement with what is being said. If the person asks "Don't you agree?" You can respond: "My only purpose right now is to try to fully understand your position and feelings about this."

• **When there is much input, "mirror back" what you have heard to check your understanding—for example: "As I understand it, you did this, because..." or, "You feel that you have been unfairly accused, because ..."**

Actually, the term "much input" should be expanded to say: "much, or complex, or ambiguous input."

This learning point must be used with discretion. It would be inappropriate to mirror back every statement that a person makes. On the other hand, you should use mirroring if you are in doubt about what was said or there is a chance that you missed important details.

In addition, you should use mirroring when a person seems confused or inconsistent. Hearing a difficult or confused thought played back from another source can have a beneficial effect on one's thinking.

Appropriate mirroring also provides reassurance to a person that you really do understand his or her position and feelings.

• **When needed, set a specific date for a follow-up meeting to permit you to collect information from other sources and/or to prepare for the next module, *Remedial Action*.**

At times, you can go right into the remedial-action phase. However, there are other times when it would be prudent to confirm the information provided by just one person, or to gather other viewpoints which might alter your perception of the situation. When this is the case, time permitting, you should check with other sources and set a specific date for a follow-up meeting.

But *for this exercise*, you must try to resolve the situation with the information at hand, *not* delay action for further investigation as is often appropriate in real-life implementation.

## Discussion of the Remedial Action Learning Points

Note: This module should be preceded by the *Nonjudgmental Information Gathering* module, and only one problem should be dealt with at a time, so that the interviewer can remain better focused and have a better chance of achieving constructive closure.

• **State any solution requirements person may not be aware of.**

It can be frustrating and time wasting to develop a "solution" that cannot be used due to technical, policy, or other constraints.

Furthermore, there are times when an enumeration of *all* requirements will turn up conflicts or competing priorities that will have to be resolved before the present problem can be dealt with effectively.

If you have any doubt about the possession of this knowledge on the part of the person you are dealing with (or yourself), clearly determine and spell out the requirements that a solution must satisfy.

- **If a simple solution is not apparent, solicit and record person's ideas for solving the problem (on a blackboard or flipchart where both of you can see them)—giving no evaluation on your part at this time.**

If a good solution to a relatively simple problem is rather obvious, there is no need to put it on display. When this is not the case, you can best encourage the other person to share his or her thinking—and be creative—by having him or her contribute *first,* and by *not* evaluating this input at this point.

- **Add your ideas—without evaluating them—then add any additional ones that occur to either of you.**

Your creativity will also benefit from adherence to this deferred evaluation rule.

Seeing the items on display can stimulate both of you to develop additional ideas to add. They need not be completely original, for originality is less important than producing a good, mutually acceptable solution. It is productive to build on each other's thinking.

- **Discuss and evaluate the ideas in terms of "pros" and "cons" associated with each (including the option of "no action").**

An acceptable solution must satisfy all constraints. In addition, it must be evaluated in terms of any weights or priorities that have been established.

If two solutions are equally acceptable to you, go with the one that is most acceptable to the other person.

Often, we fail to deal with "no action" as an alternative solution that needs to be evaluated. This is a mistake. Whatever the reason for assuming a "no action" course, it will have effects that will be just as real as those for an "action" course.

- **Seek agreement on a solution and spell out the specific steps to be taken by either, or both, of you. If you cannot agree, and you have supervisory authority over the person, specify the action you will require, your reasons for requiring it, and when you expect it to occur *(then skip the next step).***

Unless the problem was merely a misunderstanding, it will not be solved until words are converted into action.

Research findings show that "do your best" action goals are not as motivating as ones that are specific, challenging, understood, and accepted.

- **Mirror back what other is committed to (as a check on understanding; for example, saying: "As I understand it, you will do such and such"—accurately playing back what you have heard).**

- **Agree on a specific, follow-up meeting, or observation time and date, for reviewing progress or results.**

The setting of a follow-up time and date for observation (checking on results), or a meeting, assures a basis for determining whether or not the problem is really solved.

It also provides a definite basis for establishing accountability for remedial action, and it is a form of goal setting that will better motivate you and the other person to follow through on your commitments.

In addition, a definite meeting time and date assures that the person will have access to you—it will be on your calendar—and she or he will not have to worry about when and if to intrude on your busy schedule. Saying, "Check with me in 2 weeks," is far more likely to lead to delay or total forgetting.

An exception to this, of course, is when the person works in the same office with you every day. Then, you may need only a "reminder" note on your calendar to deal with the matter.

- **Praise the person as soon as possible after successful implementation occurs (or for completion of a first step in a series of steps).**

Research in behavior management shows that the timing of positive reinforcement has an important effect on its motivational value: the sooner after the desired behavior or event, the better.

In addition, research findings show that *specificity* and *location* are important:

- you should be quite specific about what you are giving praise for;
- the first and primary place for giving the praise should be the person's work station rather than the water cooler, the lunch counter, or some other place.

True, the above guidelines for giving praise may seem trivial or illogical, but there is abundant evidence that we are not as rational as we like to believe: Giving praise at the water cooler, will tend to subconsciously, reinforce going to the water cooler!

### *Show the Modeling Demonstration*

If, preferably, a videotape is used, it is important that the copy of the tape used for this first showing *not* have the learning points narrated or printed under the scenes where they occur. We want the trainees to be actively involved in determining if and "where" each learning point occurs.

Instructor: "We're going to see demonstration modeling of the learning points now. Whenever you see one of the learning points being used, make a checkmark in the space provided by it on your *Learning Points Worksheet*. If you also have time to note *where* it occurs in the roleplay, do so. "

At the end of the demonstration, have the trainees compare notes about which learning points were used, and where they were used. If there is disagreement, show the demonstration again to resolve the matter. (Needless to say, it will be helpful if you know where each learning point is used and can point this out during the repetition).

### *(Optional) After Reaching Agreement*

If the demonstration is by videotape, show a second copy with the learning points identified (via narration and/or printing beneath the scenes), to reinforce this phase of learning.

Stress the idea that the trainees should not try to passively imitate or "ape" the modeled behavior in their upcoming practice sessions—that they should utilize their own personal style and language in applying the learning points. In addition, stress their need to exercise some discretion in using them, as in deciding when it is useful to "mirror back" what the other has said.

## Phase Two Activity

On a flipchart, blackboard, or flipchart page attached to the wall, display the assignments (you have previously made) of trainees to each of the three-person and four-person practice groups, and indicate where each group should meet, and at what time they should all return to the main meeting room.

Before sending them to their practice locations, remind them that:

- The trainee playing Supervisor initiates the roleplay in each round (this gives her or him time to get ready and to mentally rehearse how to implement the first learning points on the *Learning Point Refresher Sheet*, which she or he should have in view for handy reference).
- Trainees should get into the first roleplay right off, without any preliminary discussion about behavior modeling. It will be more productive for them to talk about it *after* they have tried it.
- It is very important for those acting as Observers in a four-person group to hold the roleplayers to the time limits of *8 minutes* for the roleplay and *8 minutes* for Observer feedback. Otherwise, the last-round roleplayers may be unduly rushed or not have enough time to finish.
- When there are *both* three-person and four-person groups, three-person groups members can afford to take an additional 5 minutes per round or, when they finish, they can watch still-active, four-person groups as non-feedback-giving observers. (Optional): These "visitors" may also complete an *Observer Form* each round to compare (silently) with the feedback they hear from the assigned Observers. You will need to duplicate and distribute additional *Observer Forms* for this purpose.

- You—or your assistant(s)—should briefly visit all groups to answer any questions and observe.
    - Initially, it is important for you to check to see that each group has started promptly.
    - In subsequent visits, you should check to see if the Observers are implementing the post-roleplay steps listed on the *Observer Form* in the prescribed sequence:
        - It is especially important for them to get the reactions of the person playing Subordinate *before* possible contamination of his or her perceptions by the views of the Observer(s) and/or the stated intentions of the person playing Supervisor.
        - It is equally important for the person playing Supervisor to learn from the Subordinate and Observers how he or she "came across" before he or she has the opportunity to influence their perceptions.

Caution: Occasionally, a trainee will be unable to properly execute a learning point (such as mirroring a disliked opinion without showing disapproval) due to a strong emotional block—not because of a failure to understand it or appreciate the need to implement it. Since compliance may currently be beyond the person's control, you should discourage any disparaging remarks or coercive efforts to make the trainee "keep trying."

## Phase Three Activity

When all groups have completed their roleplay practice, trainees should convene again as a single group for you to:

- (Optional) Share some positive observations from your visits to the practicing groups,
- Answer questions (see "Possible Comments, Questions, and Answers" section below),
- Conduct a general discussion of the training experience,
- Give the homework assignment (discussed below), which requires the trainees to use the *Nonjudgmental Information Gathering* and *Remedial Action* learning points on the job, followed by completion of a *Learning Points Worksheet* and the *Homework Assignment Sheet*. Set a follow-up meeting date that will give the trainees reasonable opportunity to complete this assignment.
- (Optional) Express your willingness to meet one-on-one with any trainee before the follow-up meeting to answer additional questions, replay the *Demonstration Videotape*, and/or provide additional role-play practice in using the learning points.
- Have the trainees complete, anonymously, the *End-of-Practice-Session Questionnaire*. To assure their anonymity, ask them to print their answers, omit their names, and insert their completed forms face-down in a pile on the table. Do not collect them until all have been submitted and the pile has been shuffled.

### *Possible Comments, Questions, and Answers*

You might elaborate on a basic underlying theme of supervisory skills learning points—maintenance of the interviewee's self-esteem—by listing the following suggestions:

- hold sessions in private;
- have your secretary hold calls;
- rise when the person enters;
- leave your desk to sit with the person; and
- at the end of a session, mention some of the person's positive attributes and express confidence in his/her ability to do what needs to be done.

These measures supplement the learning points in helping to create an accepting, rather than threatening, environment. You might also mention some key assumptions that underlie the learning points:

- We should focus on evaluating overt, observable behavior, not the person.
- Effective diagnosis, remedial action, and good relations are undermined when conclusions about the causes and the effects of behavior are reached prematurely, without the benefit of readily available information.
- Most employees—when they understand and accept the nature of a work-related problem and the constraints that a solution must satisfy—will welcome an opportunity to deal with it constructively.
- A supervisor does not abandon the right to act unilaterally by attempting a collaborative approach first, and whether or not the subordinate cooperates, the supervisor will gain greater credibility and acceptance from her or his group for any unilateral corrective action that must be taken.

A trainee may complain that real-life situations are more complicated than the ones assigned in the Rolesets, and/or that there would be more information to rely on in a real-life situation.

With regard to the first point, you might observe that we benefit from trying a new skill in a simple, more manageable situation, rather than in a more difficult one. This helps us to focus on the principles involved and to avoid undue initial discouragement.

With regard to the second issue: Yes, there probably will be more information to rely on in a real-life situation. In fact, one of the learning points that we don't use in practice (about collecting additional information from other sources) was designed with this in mind. However, the assigned Rolesets do permit meaningful initial experimentation with most of the learning points, and the trainee-submitted Role-plays for subsequent practice will be associated with much more information (as will, of course, on-the-job practice).

On occasion, a trainee will express concern about this type of training: "Is it really ethical to make a conscious effort to change another person's behavior?" My response is that conscientious parents, friends, teachers, ministers—as well as supervisors—have been trying to change the behavior of others since the beginning of human history; that the ethical issue has to do with the intended purpose of the influence attempt, not the influence attempt itself.

Does the influencer intend to benefit the other person (as well as self), or is the influencer concerned with his or her personal gain—regardless of the consequences for the other? Clearly, skillful application of the *Nonjudgmental Information Gathering* and *Remedial Action* learning points will provide important benefits for both the trainee and the supervisor.

### *Homework Assignment*

Two purposes of the written homework assignment are:

- to increase trainee motivation to transfer new skills to the work setting, and
- to provide trainees with a written record for self-management and for reporting to the group (should they elect to do so).

The assignment involves completion of a *Learning Points Worksheet* and the *Homework Assignment Sheet* for an actual, individual, on-the-job performance problem situation. However, trainees are not required to turn anything in to you.

### Overlearning Practice for Some

Some trainees may benefit from additional practice prior to the scheduled follow-up meeting. As was discussed in Part I, "overlearning" is particularly relevant for those trainees who have less-productive, but well-entrenched, ways of responding to the people they supervise. They tend to revert to their habitual ways when they return to the "real world" of the everyday work environment. Such individuals should be urged to engage in additional practice prior to the scheduled follow-up meeting.

A useful way to generate additional Roleplays for them is to have them submit completed *Roleplay Input Forms* in advance, to serve as a basis for you to develop new rolesets. Then, a training group, or groups, can be formed and managed in the same manner as for the first practice session. When trainee input is used, the author of the input should be an Observer for the round in which a roleplay from it is used, to assure greater benefit to the roleplayers.

## The Follow-up Meeting

Hold a follow-up meeting after trainees have had adequate time to implement the homework assignment. There are several objectives for this meeting:

- to give trainees the opportunity to share their experiences in using the learning points (by making voluntary reports based on their completed *Learning Points Worksheets* and *Homework Assignment Sheet*(s));
- to discuss any general questions they have about using the learning points;
- to let a trainee who had difficulties in a particular interview about a performance problem observe the proper implementation of the learning points:
  - Invite him or her to verbally describe the problem situation (only as it was initially perceived by the supervisor), and to play the role of the Subordinate, with a group member volunteer assuming the role of Supervisor.
  - Unlike the procedure for practice sessions that utilize trainer-provided rolesets, the person playing Supervisor should be given the option of delaying action for "further investigation" before using the *Remedial Action* learning points.
  - If the Supervisor chooses this option, the roleplay should stop, and the trainee playing the Subordinate (who is the author of this real-life situation) now serves as an objective source to supply whatever information the Supervisor requests that he or she would have been reasonably able to obtain over the period of time that would have been available for investigation.
  - Then, the roleplay resumes with the Supervisor implementing the *Remedial Action* learning points
- to strengthen the commitment of trainees to implementation of the learning points, urge them to carry the *Learning Points Refresher Sheet* with them until the learning points become "second-nature," and schedule additional follow-up meetings as long as the trainees want them.

Good Tool: Make and distribute cards of the *Learning Points Refresher Sheet* on a small card that can be carried in a purse or wallet.

## Stimulating and Maintaining a Felt Need for Training

Some supervisors have a strong-felt need to sharpen their supervisory skills, even when they are already good or outstanding. Others, with much greater need, may resist awareness of the need, due to the distorting effects of various psychological defense mechanisms.

Studies show that anonymous, pretraining feedback from subordinates is effective in correcting such misconceptions. A useful way to get such feedback was described in Part I: ask assembled subordinates to print their responses to the following questions on 3 × 5 cards: "What should your supervisor start doing, stop doing, do less of, do more of, do differently?" (and then insert the cards, face down, in a collection pile). Alternatively, you could have them drop the cards in a locked, slotted box placed at a nonmonitored location.

In the case of candidates for supervisory positions, they might be told that, as supervisors, they will be required to periodically collect, and build upon such feedback. This can help to eliminate undesirable candidates, up front, and gain greater acceptance for this useful—though threatening to some—activity on the part of those who are appointed.

Finally, both managerial and trainee personnel need to know what was pointed out in Part I: that there can be a delay of weeks or months between positive changes in supervisory behavior and significant "bottom-line" payoffs in quality and productivity. In fact, performance may temporarily drop before it surges ahead. These "lagged effects" are well-documented by research findings.[2] Awareness of them will help you to:

- develop realistic expectations on the part of those affected,
- select a more realistic time frame in which to assess the "bottom-line" effects of the training,
- dramatize the need for revising the reward-penalty system, so that it will focus on desired supervisory behavior change in the short-term, even when it is *not* accompanied by an immediate improvement in performance (assuming that you have validated the longer-term benefits of the behavior through your assessment activity).

## Formal Evaluation of Training

If you plan to formally evaluate the effects of training, you should plan for it in advance, as you will need to take adequate "before" and "after" *behavior samples* with which to indicate the extent of behavior change.

Though we know that people have strong tendencies toward being kind, selfish, assertive, and so on, this does not show up very well when we compare only two samples of their behavior taken on different occasions. However, when we take a bigger sample—say we use the average score for five samples on each occasion—then the tendency is rather clear cut.[3] Review the Part I section on Evidence of Effectiveness.

### Collecting "Before" and "After" Samples for Trainees Who Have Subordinates

Through the use of *Questionnaire A*, you should collect "before training" scores from the trainees' subordinates for *at least* five occasions when the supervisor trainee met with a subordinate about a performance problem involving the subordinate.

*What to Do:*

- When feasible, arrange to meet with the trainees' subordinates as a large group (or hold separate meetings with each trainee's group of subordinates).
- Take enough copies of *Questionnaire A* to distribute to those who need more than one copy.
- Explain that your purpose is to obtain accurate information about aspects of their supervisor's present behavior as a basis for evaluating the effects of a training program upon that behavior:
    - that the information will not be shown to their supervisor;
    - that they should print their answers, omit their names, and insert their completed questionnaires in a pile and shuffle them to assure their anonymity; and
    - invite and answer questions.
- Have them complete *Questionnaire A* during the meeting. Explain that you will not examine or collect the pile of completed questionnaires until all have been inserted.
- After the meeting, compute an average "before" score for each Learning Point for each supervisor trainee.
- After the training—and after sufficient time has elapsed to provide an adequate sample of "performance problem" interviews—repeat the above process (using *Questionnaire B*) to compute an average "after" score for each Learning Point.

  Note: You must specify an end-of-training date when you distribute *Questionnaire B*, so that subordinates will not describe a pretraining situation (see the mention of this date specification in the *Questionnaire B* instructions).

If a group meeting with subordinates is not feasible, an alternative approach is to distribute questionnaire copies with the above explanations, instructing the subordinates to drop the completed ones in a slotted, locked box that you will provide at a nonmonitored location.

### Collecting "Before" and "After" Samples for Trainees Who Do Not Have Subordinates

You can recruit several nontrainee observers to evaluate the degree to which the trainees apply the learning points on different "before being provided with the learning points and training" roleplays and "after-training" roleplays (other than the roleplays used for their training sessions).

The after-training roleplays should require application of the same learning points as the before-training ones, and they should present the same level of difficulty. You can check for such equivalence by getting the opinions of trained individuals who roleplay both the pretraining and the posttraining ones, coupled with observer feedback about which learning points they used.

### Study End-of-Practice-Session Data

It is important to know how participants perceive their training experience as a basis for making constructive improvements to the program. Collation of the anonymous response data obtained with the *End-of-Practice-Session Questionnaire* serves this purpose.

## Forms Provided in the Trainee Manual Appendix

| | |
|---|---|
| *Learning Points Worksheet* | (5 copies) |
| *Learning Points Refresher Sheet* | (1) |
| *Observer Form* | (6 |
| *End-of-Practice-Session Questionnaire* | (4) |
| *Homework Assignment Sheet* | (4) |
| *Roleplay Input Form* | (4) |

## Notes

1. See E. A. Fleishman, "Leadership Climate, Human Relations Training, and Supervisory Behavior," *Personnel Psychology,* 1953, *5,* 205-222; R. J. House, "Leadership Training: Some Dysfunctional Consequences," *Administrative Science Quarterly,* 1968, 12, 556-571; A. A. Huczynski and J. W. Lewis, "An Empirical Study Into the Learning Transfer Process in Management Training," *Journal of Management Studies,* 1980, 17, 227-240.

2. See R. Likert, *The Human Organization: Its Management and Value.* New York: McGraw-Hill, 1967; R. Likert and J. Likert, *New Ways of Managing Conflict.* New York: McGraw-Hill, 1976; A. J. Marrow, D. G. Bowers, and S. E. Seashore, *Management By Participation.* New York: Harper and Row, 1967; J. C. Taylor and D. G. Bowers, *Survey of Organizations: Toward a Machine-Scored, Standardized Questionnaire Instrument.* Ann Arbor: Institute for Social Research, University of Michigan, 1972.

3. S. Epstein, "The Stability of Behavior: On Predicting Most of the People Much of the Time," *Journal of Personality and Social Psychology,* 1979, 37, 1097-1126.

# Appendix A
# All Forms

# Learning Points Worksheet

| *Learning Points* | *Make checkmark (below) each time the Learning Point is used* |
|---|---|
| *Explain, specifically, what you are concerned about and why you think it is a problem,* presenting any objective evidence you have, while withholding judgment of the person | |
| *Listen nonjudgmentally—to give person full opportunity to explain events and/or feelings*—and encourage responding with comments, such as, "I see," "Can you tell me more about such and such," and "What happened then?" | |
| *When there is much input, "mirror back" what you have heard* to check your understanding—for example: "As I understand it, you did this because ..." or, "You feel that you have been unfairly accused because ..." | |
| *When needed, set a specific date for a follow-up meeting,* to permit you to collect information from other sources and/or to prepare for the next module, *Remedial Action* | (not applicable in practice session) |

***Note:*** For this exercise, the person playing supervisor must try to resolve the situation with the information at hand, not delay action for further investigation, as is often appropriate in real-life implementation.

(Begin *Remedial Action* learning points)

| | |
|---|---|
| *State any solution requirements person may not be aware of* | |
| *If a simple solution is not apparent, solicit and record person's ideas for solving problem* (on a blackboard or flipchart where both of you can see them)—giving no evaluation on your part at this time | |
| *Add your ideas—without evaluating them—then add any additional ones that occur to either of you* | |
| *Discuss and evaluate the ideas in terms of "pros" and "cons" associated with each* (including the option of "no action") | |
| *Seek agreement on a solution and spell out specific steps to be taken by either or both of you.* If you cannot agree and you have supervisory authority over the person, specify the action you will require, your reasons for requiring it, and when you expect it to occur | |
| *When there is much input, "mirror back" what other is committed to* as a check on understanding; for example, saying "As I understand it, you will do such and such" | |
| *Agree on a specific follow-up meeting or observation time and date* for reviewing progress or results | |
| *Praise person as soon as possible after successful implementation occurs* (or for completion of a first step in a series of steps) | (not applicable in practice session) |

# Roleplay Input Form

Your Name ____________________

After getting acquainted with behavior modeling through the roleplays provided, it is important for you to practice applying the learning points to the types of real-life situations *you* are most likely to encounter. Think of a challenging individual, performance-problem situation that you have experienced, or observed, and *describe it below for those who will play the Supervisor and the Subordinate.*

Nature of subordinate's duties/responsibilities: ____________________

Describe subordinate's work environment: ____________________

Nature of the performance problem from the subordinate's viewpoint and knowledge at the time (if the subordinate was aware of a problem):

Describe the nature of the performance problem from the supervisor's viewpoint and knowledge at the time (regarding quality or quantity of work, tardiness, absenteeism, working with others, etc.):

Give any objective evidence the supervisor had to document the existence of the problem:

If the supervisor had previously talked to this subordinate about deficient performance, explain

# Observer Form

When you act as an *Observer*:

- Remind the person playing Supervisor to *mentally rehearse* (briefly) how s/he will implement the learning points before s/he starts the roleplay.
- As the roleplay takes place, *use the form below* to indicate by each of the learning points whether or not s/he implemented it. (Note: "Did not apply is an option on all but the first two scales).
- Check how well the roleplayers comply with the assumptions of their roles as indicated by the descriptions in your *Roleset*. (Each player received one of these descriptions.)
- Keep time, to see that the roleplay does not take more than 8 minutes, so that subsequent-round roleplayers will not be shortchanged.

See additional instructions after the Learning Points

| | *Did Not Apply* | *Yes* | *No* | *Somewhat* |
|---|---|---|---|---|
| Initially, s/he explained the performance concern objectively, without prematurely judging interviewee or being critical. | ____ | ____ | ____ | ____ |
| S/he gave interviewee ample opportunity to explain what happened and/or express feelings. | ____ | ____ | ____ | ____ |
| When appropriate, s/he summarized or "played back" what interviewee had said. | ____ | ____ | ____ | ____ |
| S/he set a specific date for a follow-up meeting to permit further data collection or preparation for solving the problem. | ____ | ____ | ____ | ____ |
| S/he stated solution requirements that interviewee was not aware of. | ____ | ____ | ____ | ____ |
| In a noncritical and friendly way, s/he solicited and recorded interviewee's ideas first for solving the problem. | ____ | ____ | ____ | ____ |
| S/he presented his/her ideas for solving the problem (after the interviewee). | ____ | ____ | ____ | ____ |
| Together, they evaluated the "pros" and "cons" of each idea (this could include the choice of "no action"). | ____ | ____ | ____ | ____ |
| They agreed on a solution that made clear any steps to be taken by each. | ____ | ____ | ____ | ____ |
| S/he summarized what interviewee was committed to do (to avoid any misunderstanding). | ____ | ____ | ____ | ____ |
| They agreed on a specific time and date for a follow-up meeting (or assessment of results). | ____ | ____ | ____ | ____ |
| At the end of the interview, s/he felt there was a problem. Though they had ample discussion, they could not agree on a solution. Then s/he explained explicitly what interviewee would have to do. | ____ | ____ | ____ | ____ |

When the Roleplay ends: Eight minutes total is allocated for the activities below (whether performed by one or two observers). ***IMPORTANT***: Perform activities in the order given.

1. Ask the person playing the Subordinate:

   - What in the interview seemed most helpful to you?
   - Was there anything negative?
   - What would you do as a result of the interview?

2. Indicate to the person playing Supervisor:

   - Any applicable learning points that were overlooked, or were implemented at the wrong time.
   - Extent to which s/he came across as being sincere.
   - Praise for learning points that were well executed (indicating the specific ones).

3. Solicit reactions from the person playing Supervisor.

*Note:* If the full 16 minutes for the round has not been used by the end of the Supervisor's comments, s/he may want to use the remaining time to repeat a specific part of the interview that was deficient.

# Homework Assignment Sheet

*Homework Assignment:* Before the scheduled follow-up meeting, apply the learning points to at least one new on-the-job, performance-problem situation. (The *Learning Points Refresher Sheet* can serve as a handy reminder during the interview.)

Immediately after the interview, complete a *Learning Points Worksheet*. Record your reactions by each learning point you used, noting your experience with it and its a effectiveness in the interaction.

What was the performance problem you dealt with? ______________________________

______________________________________________________________________

______________________________________________________________________

What was the person's apparent reaction to the interview ______________________________

______________________________________________________________________

Did the person carry out what s/he agreed to do?

| | | |
|---|---|---|
| ____ No action to be taken | ____ Too early to assess | ____ No |
| ____ Yes, very well | ____ Yes, moderately well | ____ Yes, very poorly |

Any particular "lessons learned"? ______________________________

______________________________________________________________________

______________________________________________________________________

______________________________________________________________________

______________________________________________________________________

*Note:* This completed form, along with the accompanying *Learning Points Worksheet*, are for your records and to serve as reminders should you elect to report to the group.

YOU ARE NOT REQUIRED TO TURN ANYTHING IN

# Learning Points Refresher Sheet

(Use as a reminder for rolelplays and on the job)

| *Nonjudgmental Information Gathering* (Precedes *Remedial Action*) | *Remedial Action* |
|---|---|
| Explain specifically, what you are concerned about, and why you think it is a problem.<br><br>Listen nonjudgmentally for full explanation.<br><br>When there is much input, "mirror" what you have heard, giving no evaluation.<br><br>When further information gathering is needed, set a specific date for a follow-up meeting. | • State any solution requirements person may not be aware of.<br>• If simple solution is not apparent, solicit and record person's ideas for solving the problem, giving no evaluation.<br>• Add your ideas without evaluating them, then additional ones that occur to either of you.<br>• Discuss the pros and cons of the ideas.<br>• Seek agreement on a solution that specifies steps to be taken (if no agreement can be reached, indicate what you will require, giving reasons, and set a deadline for compliance.)<br>• "Mirror back" what other is committed to (as a check on understanding).<br>• Agree on a specific follow-up meeting or observation time and date (to review progress or results).<br>• Immediately praise person for any progress toward a goal. |

# End-of-Practice-Session Questionnaire

How do you rate the live demonstration or videotape you saw today? (Please check one)

| Unacceptable | Poor | Average | Above Average | Excellent |
|---|---|---|---|---|

Do you have any suggestions for improving it for future use?

To what extent did you feel that you were in a realistic situation as you completed your roleplay as Supervisor?

| To No Extent | Little Extent | Great Extent | Completely |
|---|---|---|---|

Have you any suggestions for improving the roleplays or for improving the procedure for using them?

What is your reaction to behavior modeling as a training approach?

Other comments or suggestions

# Questionnaire A

Name of your supervisor ______________________________ Date __________________________

*Instructions:* Do not put your name on this questionnaire, we do not want to identify you. We will not show this information to your supervisor. Please be as accurate as you can in describing his/her behavior.

Think of the last time your present supervisor felt you had a performance problem (quality or quantity of work, tardiness, absenteeism, working with others, etc.) and talked with you about it.

*Check if Applicable*:

____ My present supervisor has never had such a discussion with me.

____ My present supervisor had such a discussion with me, but I can't recall the details of his/her approach.

*If you checked one of the above, do not proceed. Turn in the questionnaire now.*

If there is at least one occasion you can adequately recall, ***indicate the extent to which he or she used each of the behaviors listed on the scales provided.***

If your present supervisor had an interview with you about a performance problem on more than one occasion and you feel you can accurately recall the details of his/her approach each time, please fill out a separate questionnaire for each occasion (ask for additional questionnaires) and number them (#1, #2, #3) in the upper right hand corner of the first page.

| | *Yes* | *No* | *Somewhat* |
|---|---|---|---|
| Initially, s/he explained the performance concern objectively, without prematurely judging me or being critical. | ____ | ____ | ____ |
| S/he gave me ample opportunity to explain what had happened and/or my feelings. | ____ | ____ | ____ |

| | *Did Not Apply* | *Yes* | *No* | *Somewhat* |
|---|---|---|---|---|
| When appropriate, s/he summarized or "played back" what I had said. | ____ | ____ | ____ | ____ |
| S/he set a specific date for a follow-up meeting to permit further data collection or preparation for solving the problem. | ____ | ____ | ____ | ____ |
| S/he stated solution requirements I was not aware of. | ____ | ____ | ____ | ____ |
| When a solution was not apparent, in a noncritical and friendly way s/he solicited and recorded my ideas for solving the problem. | ____ | ____ | ____ | ____ |
| S/he presented his/her ideas for solving the problem. | ____ | ____ | ____ | ____ |
| Together, we evaluated the "pros" and "cons" of each idea (this could include the choice of "no action"). | ____ | ____ | ____ | ____ |
| We agreed on a solution that made clear any steps to be taken by either of us. | ____ | ____ | ____ | ____ |
| S/he summarized what I was committed to do (to avoid any misunderstanding). | ____ | ____ | ____ | ____ |
| We agreed on a specific time and date for a follow-up meeting (or assessment of results). | ____ | ____ | ____ | ____ |
| Very soon after successful completion of my agreed-to action, s/he praised or commended me for it. | ____ | ____ | ____ | ____ |
| At the end of our interview, s/he felt there was a problem. Though we had ample discussion, we could not agree on a solution. Then s/he told me explicitly what I would have to do. | ____ | ____ | ____ | ____ |

# Questionnaire B

Name of your supervisor ______________________________ Date ______________________________

*Instructions:* Do not put your name on this questionnaire; we do not want to identify you. We will not show this information to your supervisor. Please be as accurate as you can in describing his/her behavior.

Think of the last time ***since the date specified with the distribution of this questionnaire*** your present supervisor felt you had a performance problem (quality or quantity of work, tardiness, absenteeism, working with others, etc.) and talked with you about it.

*Check if applicable:*

____ My present supervisor has not had such a discussion with me since the specified date

***If you checked the above, do not proceed. Turn in the questionnaire now.***

If there is at least one occasion you can adequately recall, ***indicate the extent to which he or she used each of the behaviors listed on the scales provided.***

If your present supervisor had an interview with you about a performance problem on more than one occasion ***since the date specified***, please fill out a separate questionnaire for each occasion (ask for additional questionnaires) and number them (#1, #2, #3) in the upper right hand corner of the first page.

| | *Yes* | *No* | *Somewhat* |
|---|---|---|---|
| Initially, s/he explained the performance concern objectively, without prematurely judging me or being critical. | ____ | ____ | ____ |
| S/he gave me ample opportunity to explain what had happened and/or my feelings. | ____ | ____ | ____ |

| | *Did Not Apply* | *Yes* | *No* | *Somewhat* |
|---|---|---|---|---|
| When appropriate, s/he summarized or "played back" what I had said. | ____ | ____ | ____ | ____ |
| S/he set a specific date for a follow-up meeting to permit further data collection or preparation for solving the problem. | ____ | ____ | ____ | ____ |
| S/he stated solution requirements I was not aware of. | ____ | ____ | ____ | ____ |
| When a solution was not apparent, in a noncritical and friendly way s/he solicited and recorded my ideas for solving the problem. | ____ | ____ | ____ | ____ |
| S/he presented his/her ideas for solving the problem. | ____ | ____ | ____ | ____ |
| Together, we evaluated the "pros" and "cons" of each idea (this could include the choice of "no action"). | ____ | ____ | ____ | ____ |
| We agreed on a solution that made clear any steps to be taken by either of us. | ____ | ____ | ____ | ____ |
| S/he summarized what I was committed to do (to avoid any misunderstanding). | ____ | ____ | ____ | ____ |
| We agreed on a specific time and date for a follow-up meeting (or assessment of results). | ____ | ____ | ____ | ____ |
| Very soon after successful completion of my agreed-to action, s/he praised or commended me for it. | ____ | ____ | ____ | ____ |
| At the end of our interview, s/he felt there was a problem. Though we had ample discussion, we could not agree on a solution. Then s/he told me explicitly what I would have to do. | ____ | ____ | ____ | ____ |

# Appendix B

# Rolesets for Four-Person Groups

## Roleset for Group Member W

### Exercise Instructions

*Important:* You will play the roles of "supervisor," "subordinate," and "observer" in four roleplay rounds that deal will an individual performance problem. To enhance realism, and help you to get the most from your practice, ***do not look at each other's rolesets until after the roleplay practice***.

The sequence of events for your first practice session is as follows:

1. In a prepractice meeting of all trainees, your Instructor will invite questions and discussion about the learning points.
2. As you watch a live demonstration or videotaped roleplay, you will be asked to check on a *Learning Points Worksheet* whenever any learning points occur. Then, your Instructor will invite you to compare notes with other group members as to where and when they occur and discuss any discrepancies.
3. You will go to your assigned group and place for roleplay practice, during which, your Instructor (or an Instructor Assistant) will visit your group to check on progress and answer any questions.
4. After roleplay practice, all groups will reconvene with the Instructor for comments, questions, and further instructions.

In one round, you will play the role of Supervisor; in another, the role of Subordinate; and in two others, the role of Observer. Study the requirements of each role carefully. ***Each of you will gain the most, if all of you are well prepared for all three roles.***

The information provided has been kept relatively simple and limited, so that your primary focus can be on implementing the learning points. ***Do not read important events into your role; for example, do not assume a bad past relationship, or that a strike has occurred, if such information is not explicitly mentioned.***

Study your supervisory role in this roleset. Think about how you might use the learning points in dealing with your "subordinate" in the roleplay. They should not be used mechanically—they are "tools" to apply with understanding and discretion, utilizing your own personal style. As a reminder, have the *Learning Points Refresher Sheet* before you when it is your turn to be Supervisor.

Study your role as Subordinate. Imagine the feelings this person might have, and practice expressing them before the roleplay.

Study the requirements of your role as Observer on the *Observer Form* (that you will fill in as you observe a roleplay). ***It is very important that you follow the three, postroleplay steps in the sequence presented.***

### First Round

*Your Role (Supervisor):* Your name is *Robin Smith*. Three months ago you were appointed plant manager of an electronics firm that is coping with strong international competition and fast-changing technology and products. Previously, the company made lower-tech, standard products, and the demands on management and the workforce were more predictable and less challenging than they are now. You employ about 150 skilled and semiskilled workers who report to seven supervisors. You were one of these supervisors before being promoted.

Prior to the promotion, you knew that one of the average-performing peer supervisors, *Carol Young* (now your subordinate), had begun to perform at a below-satisfactory level when the company shifted to its present, higher-tech activity. You had hoped and expected that Carol's unit would have gotten up to speed by now, but this hasn't happened. This assessment is based on *objective data* which permit direct comparisons with other departments that have the same resources in relation to workload.

From your knowledge and observations of Carol, you think that s/he has the technical knowledge and experience to be a good manager. However, you have observed that Carol:

- schedules new work poorly,
- is viewed as being cool and aloof by subordinates,
- has started coercing workers to put in unexpected overtime,
- fails to keep you informed of problems until they become crises (as s/he did with your predecessor).

Carol is currently your key problem. As far as you know, s/he has no serious personal, physical, mental, financial, or family problems.

Your other supervisors are doing an excellent job; in fact, you have been commended by headquarters for the manner in which the plant has performed and adapted to new demands. However, adaptation to the new conditions has been difficult for all of the supervisors in varying degrees, and you know that Carol is well-liked by them and has their sympathy.

***You have asked Carol to stop by your office to see you. Have your* Learning Points Refresher Card *before you, and mentally rehearse what you will do.***

***When you are ready, start the roleplay.***

## SECOND ROUND

***Your Role (Observer):*** Consult your *Observer Form* for instructions. The roles you will observe (as given to the roleplayers) are:

***(Supervisor):*** Your name is *Jerry Brown*. You are the supervisor of a group of head nurses and you have just about exhausted your patience with one of them, *Chris Neely*. Chris used to be quite competent, but has fallen down on the job in the last 2 months. S/he puts off making important decisions, is increasingly neglectful of routine reports and duties, and seems generally unenthusiastic about his job. In fact, Chris's group is one of the least productive, based on several objective performance measures.

When you discussed Chris's deteriorating performance with him/her 3 weeks ago, s/he promised quite sincerely to do better. However, there has been no improvement and the morale among his/her nurses is low. Could it be that Chris thinks that long service has its entitlements, since s/he is just 3 years from retirement and knows that the hospital prides itself on looking after long-service employees? Maybe Chris thinks s/he can coast because s/he has some influential friends on the medical staff?

Chris lives alone and, as far as you know, has no other resources to live on. However, you cannot have a double standard for your head nurses. If necessary, you are now ready to consider termination. ***You have called Chris in for a talk.***

***(Subordinate):*** Your name is *Chris Neely*. You have been a head nurse for a long time; in fact, lately you've felt it has been too long. You have lost interest in supervising others and in things in general. You have the feeling that everything is uphill and sort of hopeless.

You used to be a very competent head nurse. Now, supervisory responsibilities cause you to be anxious to the point that you have trouble sleeping at night. You find it difficult to make decisions that you once found easy to make. And you have become even more concerned and anxious since you promised your supervisor, Jerry Brown, several weeks ago that you would make every effort to improve. Yet, since then, you have actually gotten worse. Your group is now very low in both objectively measured performance and morale.

You would like to get out of your present job, but to do what? The way things are going, you wonder if you could handle an ordinary nurse's job until you are eligible to retire in 3 years. Given your nontransferable retirement credits, you would lose too much by leaving the hospital now. You live alone, have no one to turn to, and have no alternative assets to live on. Your retirement payments and social security will be just adequate.

Given your many years of good, faithful service, you feel strongly that it would be quite unfair if they try to throw you out in the street. In fact, if they do, you will appeal to some influential doctors on the medical staff whom you know well and think owe you for past accommodations you have made.

***Your supervisor, Jerry Brown, has called you in for a talk and you feel very apprehensive.***

## THIRD ROUND

***Your Role (Subordinate):*** Your name is *Jo James*. You are a highly skilled and experienced maintenance worker in a textile mill who fixes machines for the production workers. You pride yourself on your outstanding diagnostic and repair abilities. It makes you feel good when you are able to get the machines going again quickly, so that the operators will not lose potential earnings due to downtime (they are on a piece-rate, incentive-pay system, and many of them have become personal friends through the years).

Your new boss, *Lane Thomas*, was transferred from the payroll office and has had no experience with maintenance work. On several occasions, s/he has observed that an increasing number of machines break down shortly after you repair them. S/he made some kind of crack about "the machines evidently being afraid of you because they're having nervous breakdowns." Perhaps s/he was trying to be funny, but you're not sure, and you feel somewhat put out with this kind of "humor."

Fact is, the likelihood of breakdown has increased significantly as the machines have aged, and this is not your fault. You can't do justice to both preventive maintenance (regular disassembly, inspection, replacement of excessively worn parts, etc.) and the provision of prompt service that operators have come to expect. Actually, providing such prompt service has become even harder as the breakdown frequency has increased. And, in your view, the basic problem is that management has failed to plan and budget for a needed preventive maintenance program; a need that was quite predictable. Of course, if they want to buy new machines, you won't mind a bit.

Your new boss's comments make you wonder if you and your hard work are really appreciated. You like the company and find your job challenging and rewarding. You would like to see the problem solved, but not at your expense. As a matter of fact, you can easily get a job elsewhere if you want to.

***Two more machines you recently repaired have just broken down and Lane Thomas has requested that you come to his/her office as soon as you are free.***

## FOURTH ROUND

***Your Role (Observer):*** Consult your *Observer Form* for instructions. The roles you will observe (as given to the roleplayers) are:

***(Supervisor):*** Your name is *Rollin Jones*. You have a very demanding job as production manager for a highly successful community, performing-arts center. You work extremely hard. Meeting deadlines, and dealing with temperamental performers and conflicting community tastes and taboos, often gets you into quite a rat race. But the satisfaction of helping to give birth to a first-class production is hard to describe.

To save money and provide "involvement opportunity" to members of the community, you utilize a group of volunteer, unpaid assistants (really "errand persons or "go-fors"). In return for free admission to shows, they do whatever needs to be done: setting up tables and chairs, running errands, washing dishes, helping with props—whatever is needed at the time. Since tickets for many of the productions are rather expensive, the assistant job is very popular. You have a large backlog of applications for it. Unfortunately, by its very nature, the work of assistants cannot be scheduled, so they often spend a lot of time sitting and waiting to be utilized. Typically, when they are needed, it's right then, and peaks in demand come unexpectedly.

One of the assistants, bright and able *Sandy Betts*, is more effective in action than most. S/he has a lot of savvy about how to do things quickly and effectively. However, Sandy strikes you as being somewhat of an irritating smart-ass. S/he acts superior to the other assistants and does not seem to respect the system and your needs. For example, the other night several assistants complained to you that Sandy was often not around when things got quite active and everyone was really needed; that s/he would be away visiting with people or just goofing off.

Later that evening, you were under the gun and up to your ears in unexpected delays and other problems. You had an urgent assignment for an assistant and none was available.

Recalling the comments about Sandy, you were pretty ticked-off. Finally, you tracked Sandy down at the bandstand. You had to rush away to another matter, but in giving him/her the assignment, you delivered a warning message loud and clear: "The other assistants are complaining about you, Sandy. Keep in mind that you can be easily replaced."

***The complaints have continued so you have sent word for Sandy to come to your office.***

***(Subordinate):*** Your name is *Sandy Betts*. You are a volunteer, unpaid, production assistant who gets to see outstanding shows free of charge for being a general "errand person" or "go-for." Since tickets for many of the productions are rather expensive, the assistant job is very popular. There is a large backlog of applications for it.

You have a lot of energy and are very conscientious with your assignments. In fact, you're more efficient than most of the other assistants. However, you wonder if your boss, *Rollin Jones* (the production manager), really appreciates your good efforts. S/he commended you once for sniffing out some "lost equipment"; yet, was obviously quite unhappy with you the other night. After tracking you down to the bandstand, Rollin muttered that other assistants were unhappy with you and that you could be easily replaced.

This shook you up a little, but you didn't have time to get an explanation, because Rollin thrust an urgent assignment on you and rushed away. However, you let it ride, feeling it was probably due to nerves before a big production, coupled with some snide comments from the other assistants, because they are jealous of your obvious ability.

Peaks in demand for "go-for" help are very unpredictable, so little of the work can be scheduled, and when you are needed, it's right then. However, just waiting for an assignment can be very boring. You like to divert yourself by seeking out performers, band members, or other interesting people to talk with. As a matter of fact, if you always had to stay in one place when there's nothing to do, you wouldn't want to keep the job.

At first, you wondered why they hadn't invested in beepers or some other type of paging equipment to facilitate communication with, and between, assistants. But you doubt that they'd be interested in what lowly assistants think. Furthermore, you doubt that they would be willing to spend the money.

***Your boss, Rollin Jones, has sent word for you to come by her/his office.***

## ROLESET FOR GROUP MEMBER X

### EXERCISE INSTRUCTIONS

*Important:* You will play the roles of "supervisor," "subordinate," and "observer" in four roleplay rounds that deal will an individual performance problem. To enhance realism, and help you to get the most from your practice, ***do not look at each other's rolesets until after the roleplay practice.***

The sequence of events for your first practice session is as follows:

1. In a prepractice meeting of all trainees, your Instructor will invite questions and discussion about the learning points.
2. As you watch a live demonstration or videotaped roleplay, you will be asked to check on a *Learning Points Worksheet* whenever any learning points occur. Then, your Instructor will invite you to compare notes with other group members as to where and when they occur and discuss any discrepancies.
3. You will go to your assigned group and place for roleplay practice, during which, your Instructor (or an Instructor Assistant) will visit your group to check on progress and answer any questions.
4. After roleplay practice, all groups will reconvene with the Instructor for comments, questions, and further instructions.

In one round, you will play the role of Supervisor; in another, the role of Subordinate; and in two others, the role of Observer. Study the requirements of each role carefully. ***Each of you will gain the most, if all of you are well prepared for all three roles.***

The information provided has been kept relatively simple and limited, so that your primary focus can be on implementing the learning points. ***Do not read important events into your role; for example, do not assume a bad past relationship, or that a strike has occurred, if such information is not explicitly mentioned.***

Study your supervisory role in this roleset. Think about how you might use the learning points in dealing with your "subordinate" in the roleplay. They should not be used mechanically—they are "tools" to apply with understanding and discretion, utilizing your own personal style. As a reminder, have the *Learning Points Refresher* sheet before you when it is your turn to be Supervisor.

Study your role as Subordinate. Imagine the feelings this person might have, and practice expressing them before the roleplay.

Study the requirements of your role as Observer on the *Observer Form* (that you will fill in as you observe a roleplay). ***It is very important that you follow the three, postroleplay steps in the sequence presented.***

### FIRST ROUND

***Your Role (Observer):*** Consult your *Observer Form* for instructions. The roles you will observe (as given to the roleplayers) are:

***(Supervisor):*** Your name is *Robin Smith.* Three months ago you were appointed plant manager of an electronics firm that is coping with strong international competition and fast-changing technology and products. Previously, the company made lower-tech, standard products, and the demands on management and the workforce were more predictable and less challenging than they are now. You employ about 150 skilled and semiskilled workers who report to seven supervisors. You were one of these supervisors before being promoted.

Prior to the promotion, you knew that one of the average-performing, peer supervisors, *Carol Young* (now your subordinate), had begun to perform at a below-satisfactory level when the company shifted to its present higher-tech activity. You had hoped and expected that Carol's unit would have gotten up to speed by now, but this hasn't happened. This assessment is based on *objective data* which permit direct comparisons with other departments that have the same resources in relation to workload.

From your knowledge and observations of Carol, you think that s/he has the technical knowledge and experience to be a good manager. However, you have observed that Carol:

- schedules new work poorly,
- is viewed as being cool and aloof by subordinates,
- has started coercing workers to put in unexpected overtime,
- fails to keep you informed of problems until they become crises (as she did with your predecessor).

Carol is currently your key problem. As far as you know, s/he has no serious personal physical, mental, financial, or family problems.

Your other supervisors are doing an excellent job; in fact, you have been commended by headquarters for the manner in which the plant has performed and adapted to new demands.

However, adaptation to the new conditions has been difficult for all of the supervisors in varying degrees, and you know that Carol is well-liked by them and has their sympathy. ***You have asked Carol to stop by your office to see you.***

***(Subordinate):*** Your name is *Carol Young*. You are one of seven supervisors of skilled and semiskilled workers in an electronics firm that is currently coping with strong international competition and fast-changing technology and products. You have been a supervisor for 9 years and are well-liked by the other supervisors.

Previously, when the company made lower-tech, standard products, the demands on management and the workforce were more predictable and less challenging than they are now. *Robin Smith*, a former fellow supervisor, was promoted to the position of plant manager (your boss) 3 months ago. S/he has been quite busy consolidating the plant's new mode of operation, so you've had little contact since the promotion. However, as far as you know, your relationship with him/her is okay.

You miss the greater stability and orderliness of the former mode of operating. For example, you've never been too keen about scheduling work, but at least under the old system things would tend to shake out after a little trial and error. But this has not worked too well under the new setup and the productivity of your unit has suffered. You are hesitant about asking the other less-senior supervisors for help, so you've tried to compensate for your errors by pushing your people for unexpected overtime. They don't want it and resent you for coercing them.

So, things are not going too well and the productivity of your unit, as revealed by objective comparisons with the other units that have essentially the same resources, has suffered. However, you have always believed that people should stay in their place and that they are expected to know what they are doing. Consequently, you maintain your distance from you subordinates, and you dislike troubling your boss about problems unless they really get out of hand.

During the last 3 years, there were two plant managers before Robin. They didn't seem interested in you as a person. They just kept pushing you to get your unit's output above the average level. You saw little reason for busting your butt for something you couldn't accomplish, and you weren't at all confident you would be fairly rewarded for significant increases.

***Robin Smith has asked you to drop by for a chat and you expect to get the same speech that you got from the former plant managers: that you have the technical knowledge and experience to be a better manager, but have the wrong attitude.***

## Second Round

***Your Role (Supervisor):*** Your name is *Jerry Brown*. You are the supervisor of a group of head nurses and you have just about exhausted your patience with one of them, *Chris Neely*. Chris used to be quite competent, but has fallen down on the job in the last 2 months. S/he puts off making important decisions, is increasingly neglectful of routine reports and duties, and seems generally unenthusiastic about his/her job. In fact, Chris's group is one of the least productive, based on several objective performance measures.

When you discussed Chris's deteriorating performance with him/her 3 weeks ago, s/he promised quite sincerely to do better. However, there has been no improvement and the morale among his/her nurses is low. Could it be that Chris thinks that long service has its entitlements, since s/he is just 3 years from retirement and knows that the hospital prides itself on looking after long-service employees? Maybe Chris thinks s/he can coast because s/he has some influential friends on the medical staff?

Chris lives alone and, as far as you know, has no other resources to live on. However, you cannot have a double standard for your head nurses. If necessary, you are now ready to consider termination.

***You have called Chris in for a talk.***

***Have your* Learning Points Refresher Card *before you, and mentally rehearse what you will do.***

***When you are ready, start the roleplay.***

## Third Round

***Your Role (Observer):*** Consult your *Observer Form* for instructions. The roles you will observe (as given to the roleplayers) are:

***(Supervisor):*** Your name is *Lane Thomas*. You were recently promoted from the payroll office of a textile mill to the position of maintenance supervisor. You supervise the maintenance workers who keep the machines going. You have had no training or experience with maintenance work, but since this involved an increase in status, pay, and visibility, you accepted it.

In giving you this new position, your boss reminded you that foreign competition is giving the company a hard time and that it is absolutely essential to cut costs to the bone. As he put it, "Maintenance expense is a nonproductive, but necessary evil; don't get any fancy ideas."

The other maintenance workers regard *Jo James* as one of the best of your crew. They say s/he is an outstanding diagnostician, works with amazing speed, and works hard. But you wonder. It seems that an increasing number of machines that Jo has just "fixed" break down soon after her intervention.

Could it be that his/her reputation with the other maintenance people is due to his/her likability, and that his/her good standing with the operators is based on "quick fixes" rather than on less superficial and more lasting repairs? (Quick fixes would minimize their downtime and lost potential earnings).

In an attempt to keep it light while communicating a subtle hint about the matter, on several occasions involving very short-lived repairs, you observed to Jo that "the machines must be afraid of him/her, because they have a nervous breakdown shortly after they see him/her." You're not sure that she took this with good humor.

In any event, the "hint" hasn't done any good, because two more recent repairs just went bad. ***You think it time to devote more attention to this problem and have asked Jo James to come by your office when s/he is free.***

***(Subordinate):*** Your name is *Jo James*. You are a highly skilled and experienced maintenance worker in a textile mill who fixes machines for the production workers. You pride yourself on your outstanding diagnostic and repair abilities. It makes you feel good when you are able to get the machines going again quickly, so that the operators will not lose potential earnings due to downtime (they are on a piece-rate, incentive-pay system, and many of them have become personal friends through the years).

Your new boss, *Lane Thomas*, was transferred from the payroll office and has had no experience with maintenance work. On several occasions, s/he has observed that an increasing number of machines break down shortly after you repair them. S/he made some kind of crack about "the machines evidently being afraid of you because they're having nervous breakdowns." Perhaps s/he was trying to be funny, but you're not sure, and you feel somewhat put out with this kind of "humor."

Fact is, the likelihood of breakdown has increased significantly as the machines have aged, and this is not your fault. You can't do justice to both preventive maintenance (regular disassembly, inspection, replacement of excessively worn parts, etc.) and the provision of prompt service that operators have come to expect. Actually, providing such prompt service has become even harder as the breakdown frequency has increased. And in your view, the basic problem is that management has failed to plan and budget for a needed preventive maintenance program; a need that was quite predictable. Of course, if they want to buy new machines, you won't mind a bit.

Your new boss's comments make you wonder if you and your hard work are really appreciated. You like the company and find your job challenging and rewarding. You would like to see the problem solved, but not at your expense. As a matter of fact, you can easily get a job elsewhere if you want to. ***Two more machines you recently repaired have just broken down and Lane Thomas has requested that you come to his/her office as soon as you are free.***

## FOURTH ROUND

***Your Role (Subordinate):*** Your name is *Sandy Betts*. You are a volunteer, unpaid, production assistant who gets to see outstanding shows free of charge for being a general "errand person" or "go-for." Since tickets for many of the productions are rather expensive, the assistant job is very popular. There is a large backlog of applications for it.

You have a lot of energy and are very conscientious with your assignments. In fact, you're more efficient than most of the other assistants. However, you wonder if your boss, *Rollin Jones* (the production manager), really appreciates your good efforts. S/he commended you once for sniffing out some "lost equipment"; yet, was obviously quite unhappy with you the other night. After tracking you down to the bandstand, Rollin muttered that other assistants were unhappy with you and that you could be easily replaced.

This shook you up a little, but you didn't have time to get an explanation, because Rollin thrust an urgent assignment on you and rushed away. However, you let it ride, feeling it was probably due to nerves before a big production coupled with some snide comments from the other assistants, because they are jealous of your obvious ability.

Peaks in demand for "go-for" help are very unpredictable, so little of the work can be scheduled, and when you are needed, it's right then. However, just waiting for an assignment can be very boring. You like to divert yourself by seeking out performers, band members, or other interesting people to talk with. As a matter of fact, if you always had to stay in one place when there's nothing to do, you wouldn't want to keep the job.

At first, you wondered why they hadn't invested in beepers or some other type of paging equipment to facilitate communication with, and between, assistants. But you doubt that they'd be interested in what lowly assistants think. Furthermore, you doubt that they would be willing to spend the money.

***Your boss, Rollin Jones, has sent word for you to come by his office.***

## Roleset for Group Member Y

### Exercise Instructions

*Important:* You will play the roles of "supervisor," "subordinate," and "observer" in four roleplay rounds that deal will an individual performance problem. To enhance realism, and help you to get the most from your practice, ***do not look at each other's rolesets until after the roleplay practice.***

The sequence of events for your first practice session is as follows:

1. In a prepractice meeting of all trainees, your Instructor will invite questions and discussion about the learning points.
2. As you watch a live demonstration or videotaped roleplay, you will be asked to check on a *Learning Points Worksheet* whenever any learning points occur. Then, your Instructor will invite you to compare notes with other group members as to where and when they occur and discuss any discrepancies.
3. You will go to your assigned group and place for roleplay practice, during which, your Instructor (or an Instructor Assistant) will visit your group to check on progress and answer any questions.
4. After roleplay practice, all groups will reconvene with the Instructor for comments, questions, and further instructions.

In one round, you will play the role of Supervisor; in another, the role of Subordinate; and in two others, the role of Observer. Study the requirements of each role carefully. ***Each of you will gain the most, if all of you are well prepared for all three roles.***

The information provided has been kept relatively simple and limited, so that your primary focus can be on implementing the learning points. ***Do not read important events into your role; for example, do not assume a bad past relationship, or that a strike has occurred, if such information is not explicitly mentioned.***

Study your supervisory role in this roleset. Think about how you might use the learning points in dealing with your "subordinate" in the roleplay. They should not be used mechanically—they are "tools" to apply with understanding and discretion, utilizing your own personal style. As a reminder, have the *Learning Points Refresher Sheet* before you when it is your turn to be Supervisor.

Study your role as Subordinate. Imagine the feelings this person might have, and practice expressing them before the roleplay.

Study the requirements of your role as Observer on the *Observer Form* (that you will fill in as you observe a roleplay). ***It is very important that you follow the three, post-roleplay steps in the sequence presented.***

### First Round

***Your Role (Subordinate):*** Your name is *Carol Young*. You are one of seven supervisors of skilled and semi-skilled workers in an electronics firm that is currently coping with strong international competition and fast-changing technology and products. You have been a supervisor for 9 years and are well-liked by the other supervisors.

Previously, when the company made lower-tech, standard products, the demands on management and the workforce were more predictable and less challenging than they are now. *Robin Smith*, a former fellow supervisor, was promoted to the position of plant manager (your boss) 3 months ago. S/he has been quite busy consolidating the plant's new mode of operation, so you've had little contact since the promotion. However, as far as you know, your relationship with him/her is okay.

You miss the greater stability and orderliness of the former mode of operating. For example, you've never been too keen about scheduling work, but at least under the old system things would tend to shake out after a little trial and error. But this has not worked too well under the new setup and the productivity of your unit has suffered. You are hesitant about asking the other less-senior supervisors for help, so you've tried to compensate for your errors by pushing your people for unexpected overtime. They don't want it and resent you for coercing them.

So, things are not going too well and the productivity of your unit, as revealed by objective comparisons with the other units that have essentially the same resources, has suffered. However, you have always believed that people should stay in their place and that they are expected to know what they are doing. Consequently, you maintain your distance from your subordinates and you dislike troubling your boss about problems unless they really get out of hand.

During the last 3 years, there were two plant managers before Robin. They didn't seem interested in you as a person. They just kept pushing you to get your unit's output above the average level. You saw little reason for busting your butt for something you couldn't accomplish, and you weren't at all confident you would be fairly rewarded for significant increases. ***Robin Smith has asked you to drop by for a chat and you expect to get the same speech that you got from the former plant managers: that you have the technical knowledge and experience to be a better manager, but have the wrong attitude.***

## SECOND ROUND

***Your Role (Observer):*** Consult your *Observer Form* for instructions. The roles you will observe (as given to the roleplayers) are:

***(Supervisor):*** Your name is *Jerry Brown*. You are the supervisor of a group of head nurses and you have just about exhausted your patience with one of them, *Chris Neely*. Chris used to be quite competent, but has fallen down on the job in the last 2 months. S/he puts off making important decisions, is increasingly neglectful of routine reports and duties, and seems generally unenthusiastic about his/her job. In fact, Chris's group is one of the least productive, based on several objective performance measures.

When you discussed Chris's deteriorating performance with him/her 3 weeks ago, s/he promised quite sincerely to do better. However, there has been no improvement and the morale among his/her nurses is low. Could it be that Chris thinks that long service has its entitlements, since s/he is just 3 years from retirement and knows that the hospital prides itself on looking after long-service employees? Maybe Chris thinks s/he can coast because s/he has some influential friends on the medical staff?

Chris lives alone and, as far as you know, has no other resources to live on. However, you cannot have a double standard for your head nurses. If necessary you are now ready to consider termination. ***You have called Chris in for a talk.***

***(Subordinate):*** Your name is *Chris Neely*. You have been a head nurse for a long time; in fact, lately you've felt it has been too long. You have lost interest in supervising others and in things in general. You have the feeling that everything is uphill and sort of hopeless.

You used to be a very competent head nurse. Now, supervisory responsibilities cause you to be anxious to the point that you have trouble sleeping at night. You find it difficult to make decisions that you once found easy to make. And you have become even more concerned and anxious since you promised your supervisor, *Jerry Brown*, several weeks ago that you would make every effort to improve. Yet, since then, you have actually gotten worse. Your group is now very low in both objectively measured performance and morale.

You would like to get out of your present job, but to do what? The way things are going, you wonder if you could handle an ordinary nurse's job until you are eligible to retire in 3 years. Given your nontransferable retirement credits, you would lose too much by leaving the hospital now. You live alone, have no one to turn to, and have no alternative assets to live on. Your retirement payments and social security will be just adequate.

Given your many years of good, faithful service, you feel strongly that it would be quite unfair if they try to throw you out in the street. In fact, if they do, you will appeal to some influential doctors on the medical staff whom you know well and think owe you for past accommodations you have made.

***Your supervisor, Jerry Brown, has called you in for a talk and you feel very apprehensive.***

## THIRD ROUND

***Your Role (Supervisor):*** Your name is *Lane Thomas*. You were recently promoted from the payroll office of a textile mill to the position of maintenance supervisor. You supervise the maintenance workers who keep the machines going. You have had no training or experience with maintenance work, but since this involved an increase in status, pay, and visibility, you accepted it.

In giving you this new position, your boss reminded you that foreign competition is giving the company a hard time and that it is absolutely essential to cut costs to the bone. As he put it, "Maintenance expense is a nonproductive, but necessary evil; don't get any fancy ideas."

The other maintenance workers regard *Jo James* as one of the best of your crew. They say s/he is an outstanding diagnostician, works with amazing speed, and works hard. But you wonder. It seems that an increasing number of machines that Jo has just "fixed" break down soon after his/her intervention.

Could it be that his/her reputation with the other maintenance people is due to his/her likability, and that his/her good standing with the operators is based on "quick fixes" rather than on less superficial and more lasting repairs? (Quick fixes would minimize their downtime and lost potential earnings.)

In an attempt to keep it light while communicating a subtle hint about the matter, on several occasions involving very short-lived repairs, you observed to Jo that "the machines must be afraid of him/her, because they have a nervous breakdown shortly after they see him/her." You're not sure that s/he took this with good humor.

In any event, the "hint" hasn't done any good, because two more recent repairs just went bad. ***You think it time to devote more attention to this problem and have asked Jo James to come by your office when s/he is free.***

***Have your* Learning Points Refresher Card *before you, and mentally rehearse what you will do.***

***When you are ready, start the roleplay.***

## Fourth Round

***Your Role (Observer):*** Consult your *Observer Form* for instructions. The roles you will observe (as given to the roleplayers) are:

***(Supervisor):*** Your name is *Rollin Jones*. You have a very demanding job as production manager for a highly successful community, performing-arts center. You work extremely hard. Meeting deadlines, and dealing with temperamental performers and conflicting community tastes and taboos, often gets you into quite a rat race. But the satisfaction of helping to give birth to a first-class production is hard to describe.

To save money and provide "involvement opportunity" to members of the community, you utilize a group of volunteer, unpaid assistants (really "errand persons or "go-fors"). In return for free admission to shows, they do whatever needs to be done: setting up tables and chairs, running errands, washing dishes, helping with props—whatever is needed at the time. Since tickets for many of the productions are rather expensive, the assistant job is very popular. You have a large backlog of applications for it. Unfortunately, by its very nature, the work of assistants cannot be scheduled, so they often spend a lot of time sitting and waiting to be utilized. Typically, when they are needed, it's right then, and peaks in demand come unexpectedly.

One of the assistants, bright and able *Sandy Betts*, is more effective in action than most. S/he has a lot of savvy about how to do things quickly and effectively. However, Sandy strikes you as being somewhat of an irritating smart-ass. S/he acts superior to the other assistants and does not seem to respect the system and your needs. For example, the other night several assistants complained to you that Sandy was often not around when things got quite active and everyone was really needed; that s/he would be away visiting with people or just goofing off.

Later that evening, you were under the gun and up to your ears in unexpected delays and other problems. You had an urgent assignment for an assistant and none was available.

Recalling the comments about Sandy, you were pretty ticked-off. Finally, you tracked Sandy down at the bandstand. You had to rush away to another matter, but in giving her the assignment, you delivered a warning message loud and clear: "The other assistants are complaining about you, Sandy. Keep in mind that you can be easily replaced."

***The complaints have continued so you have sent word for Sandy to come to your office.***

***(Subordinate):*** Your name is *Sandy Betts*. You are a volunteer, unpaid, production assistant who gets to see outstanding shows free of charge for being a general "errand person" or "go-for." Since tickets for many of the productions are rather expensive, the assistant job is very popular. There is a large backlog of applications for it.

You have a lot of energy and are very conscientious with your assignments. In fact, you're more efficient than most of the other assistants. However, you wonder if your boss, *Rollin Jones* (the production manager), really appreciates your good efforts. He commended you once for sniffing out some "lost equipment"; yet, was obviously quite unhappy with you the other night. After tracking you down to the bandstand, Rollin muttered that other assistants were unhappy with you and that you could be easily replaced.

This shook you up a little, but you didn't have time to get an explanation, because Rollin thrust an urgent assignment on you and rushed away. However, you let it ride, feeling it was probably due to nerves before a big production coupled with some snide comments from the other assistants, because they are jealous of your obvious ability.

Peaks in demand for "go-for" help are very unpredictable, so little of the work can be scheduled, and when you are needed, it's right then. However, just waiting for an assignment can be very boring. You like to divert yourself by seeking out performers, band members, or other interesting people to talk with. As a matter of fact, if you always had to stay in one place when there's nothing to do, you wouldn't want to keep the job.

At first, you wondered why they hadn't invested in beepers or some other type of paging equipment to facilitate communication with, and between, assistants. But you doubt that they'd be interested in what lowly assistants think. Furthermore, you doubt that they would be willing to spend the money.

***Your boss, Rollin Jones, has sent word for you to come by his office.***

## ROLESET FOR GROUP MEMBER Z

### EXERCISE INSTRUCTIONS

***Important:*** You will play the roles of "supervisor," "subordinate," and "observer" in four roleplay rounds that deal will an individual performance problem. To enhance realism, and help you to get the most from your practice, ***do not look at each other's rolesets until after the roleplay practice.***

The sequence of events for your first practice session is as follows:

1. In a prepractice meeting of all trainees, your Instructor will invite questions and discussion about the learning points.
2. As you watch a live demonstration or videotaped roleplay, you will be asked to check on a *Learning Points Worksheet* whenever any learning points occur. Then, your Instructor will invite you to compare notes with other group members as to where and when they occur and discuss any discrepancies.
3. You will go to your assigned group and place for roleplay practice, during which, your Instructor (or an Instructor Assistant) will visit your group to check on progress and answer any questions.
4. After roleplay practice, all groups will reconvene with the Instructor for comments, questions, and further instructions.

In one round, you will play the role of Supervisor; in another, the role of Subordinate; and in two others, the role of Observer. Study the requirements of each role carefully. ***Each of you will gain the most, if all of you are well prepared for all three roles.***

The information provided has been kept relatively simple and limited, so that your primary focus can be on implementing the learning points. ***Do not read important events into your role; for example, do not assume a bad past relationship, or that a strike has occurred, if such information is not explicitly mentioned.***

Study your supervisory role in this roleset. Think about how you might use the learning points in dealing with your "subordinate" in the roleplay. They should not be used mechanically—they are "tools" to apply with understanding and discretion, utilizing your own personal style. As a reminder, have the *Learning Points Refresher Sheet* before you when it is your turn to be Supervisor.

Study your role as Subordinate. Imagine the feelings this person might have, and practice expressing them before the roleplay.

Study the requirements of your role as Observer on the *Observer Form* (that you will fill in as you observe a roleplay). ***It is very important that you follow the three, post-roleplay steps in the sequence presented.***

### FIRST ROUND

***Your Role (Observer):*** Consult your *Observer Form* for instructions. The roles you will observe (as given to the roleplayers) are:

***(Supervisor):*** Your name is *Robin Smith.* Three months ago you were appointed plant manager of an electronics firm that is coping with strong international competition and fast-changing technology and products. Previously, the company made lower-tech, standard products, and the demands on management and the workforce were more predictable and less challenging than they are now. You employ about 150 skilled and semiskilled workers who report to seven supervisors. You were one of these supervisors before being promoted.

Prior to the promotion, you knew that one of the average-performing, peer supervisors, *Carol Young* (now your subordinate), had begun to perform at a below-satisfactory level when the company shifted to its present higher-tech activity. You had hoped and expected that Carol's unit would have gotten up to speed by now, but this hasn't happened. This assessment is based on *objective data* which permit direct comparisons with other departments that have the same resources in relation to workload.

From your knowledge and observations of Carol, you think that s/he has the technical knowledge and experience to be a good manager. However, you have observed that Carol:

- schedules new work poorly,
- is viewed as being cool and aloof by subordinates,
- has started coercing workers to put in unexpected overtime,
- fails to keep you informed of problems until they become crises (as s/he did with your predecessor).

Carol is currently your key problem. As far as you know, s/he has no serious personal physical, mental, financial, or family problems.

Your other supervisors are doing an excellent job; in fact, you have been commended by headquarters for the manner in which the plant has performed and adapted to new demands.

However, adaptation to the new conditions has been difficult for all of the supervisors in varying degrees, and you know that Carol is well-liked by them and has their sympathy. ***You have asked Carol to stop by your office to see you.***

***(Subordinate):*** Your name is *Carol Young*. You are one of seven supervisors of skilled and semiskilled workers in an electronics firm that is currently coping with strong international competition and fast-changing technology and products. You have been a supervisor for 9 years and are well-liked by the other supervisors.

Previously, when the company made lower-tech, standard products, the demands on management and the workforce were more predictable and less challenging than they are now. *Robin Smith*, a former fellow supervisor, was promoted to the position of plant manager (your boss) 3 months ago. S/he has been quite busy consolidating the plant's new mode of operation, so you've had little contact since the promotion. However, as far as you know, your relationship with him/her is okay.

You miss the greater stability and orderliness of the former mode of operating. For example, you've never been too keen about scheduling work, but at least under the old system things would tend to shake out after a little trial and error. But this has not worked too well under the new setup and the productivity of your unit has suffered. You are hesitant about asking the other less-senior supervisors for help, so you've tried to compensate for your errors by pushing your people for unexpected overtime. They don't want it and resent you for coercing them.

So, things are not going too well and the productivity of your unit, as revealed by objective comparisons with the other units that have essentially the same resources, has suffered. However, you have always believed that people should stay in their place and that they are expected to know what they are doing. Consequently, you maintain your distance from you subordinates, and you dislike troubling your boss about problems unless they really get out of hand.

During the last 3 years, there were two plant managers before Robin. They didn't seem interested in you as a person. They just kept pushing you to get your unit's output above the average level. You saw little reason for busting your butt for something you couldn't accomplish, and you weren't at all confident you would be fairly rewarded for significant increases.

***Robin Smith has asked you to drop by for a chat and you expect to get the same speech that you got from the former plant managers: that you have the technical knowledge and experience to be a better manager, but have the wrong attitude.***

## Second Round

***(Subordinate):*** Your name is *Chris Neely*. You have been a head nurse for a long time; in fact, lately you've felt it has been too long. You have lost interest in supervising others and in things in general. You have the feeling that everything is uphill and sort of hopeless.

You used to be a very competent head nurse. Now, supervisory responsibilities cause you to be anxious to the point that you have trouble sleeping at night. You find it difficult to make decisions that you once found easy to make. And you have become even more concerned and anxious since you promised your supervisor, *Jerry Brown*, several weeks ago that you would make every effort to improve. Yet, since then, you have actually gotten worse. Your group is now very low in both objectively measured performance and morale.

You would like to get out of your present job, but to do what? The way things are going, you wonder if you could handle an ordinary nurse's job until you are eligible to retire in 3 years. Given your nontransferable retirement credits, you would lose too much by leaving the hospital now. You live alone, have no one to turn to, and have no alternative assets to live on. Your retirement payments and social security will be just adequate.

Given your many years of good, faithful service, you feel strongly that it would be quite unfair if they try to throw you out in the street. In fact, if they do, you will appeal to some influential doctors on the medical staff whom you know well and think owe you for past accommodations you have made.

***Your supervisor, Jerry Brown, has called you in for a talk and you feel very apprehensive.***

## Third Round

*Your Role (Observer):* Consult your *Observer Form* for instructions. The roles you will observe (as given to the roleplayers) are:

*(Supervisor):* Your name is *Lane Thomas*. You were recently promoted from the payroll office of a textile mill to the position of maintenance supervisor. You supervise the maintenance workers who keep the machines going. You have had no training or experience with maintenance work, but since this involved an increase in status, pay, and visibility, you accepted it.

In giving you this new position, your boss reminded you that foreign competition is giving the company a hard time and that it is absolutely essential to cut costs to the bone. As he put it, "Maintenance expense is a nonproductive, but necessary evil; don't get any fancy ideas."

The other maintenance workers regard *Jo James* as one of the best of your crew. They say s/he is an outstanding diagnostician, works with amazing speed, and works hard. But you wonder. It seems that an increasing number of machines that Jo has just "fixed" break down soon after his/her intervention.

Could it be that his/her reputation with the other maintenance people is due to his/her likability, and that his/her good standing with the operators is based on "quick fixes" rather than on less superficial and more lasting repairs? (Quick fixes would minimize their downtime and lost potential earnings.)

In an attempt to keep it light while communicating a subtle hint about the matter, on several occasions involving very short-lived repairs, you observed to Jo that "the machines must be afraid of him/her, because they have a nervous breakdown shortly after they see him/her." You're not sure that s/he took this with good humor.

In any event, the "hint" hasn't done any good, because two more recent repairs just went bad. ***You think it time to devote more attention to this problem and have asked Jo James to come by your office when she is free.***

*(Subordinate):* Your name is *Jo James*. You are a highly skilled and experienced maintenance worker in a textile mill who fixes machines for the production workers. You pride yourself on your outstanding diagnostic and repair abilities. It makes you feel good when you are able to get the machines going again quickly, so that the operators will not lose potential earnings due to downtime (they are on a piece-rate, incentive-pay system, and many of them have become personal friends through the years).

Your new boss, *Lane Thomas*, was transferred from the payroll office and has had no experience with maintenance work. On several occasions, s/he has observed that an increasing number of machines break down shortly after you repair them. S/he made some kind of crack about "the machines evidently being afraid of you because they're having nervous breakdowns." Perhaps s/he was trying to be funny, but you're not sure, and you feel somewhat put out with this kind of "humor."

Fact is, the likelihood of breakdown has increased significantly as the machines have aged, and this is not your fault. You can't do justice to both preventive maintenance (regular disassembly, inspection, replacement of excessively worn parts, etc.) and the provision of prompt service that operators have come to expect. Actually, providing such prompt service has become even harder as the breakdown frequency has increased. And in your view, the basic problem is that management has failed to plan and budget for a needed preventive maintenance program; a need that was quite predictable. Of course, if they want to buy new machines, you won't mind a bit.

Your new boss's comments make you wonder if you and your hard work are really appreciated. You like the company and find your job challenging and rewarding. You would like to see the problem solved, but not at your expense. As a matter of fact, you can easily get a job elsewhere if you want to.

***Two more machines you recently repaired have just broken down and Lane Thomas has requested that you come to his/her office as soon as you are free.***

## Fourth Round

*Your Role (Supervisor):* Your name is *Rollin Jones*. You have a very demanding job as production manager for a highly successful community, performing-arts center. You work very hard. Meeting deadlines, and dealing with temperamental performers and conflicting community tastes and taboos, often gets you into quite a rat race. But the satisfaction of helping to give birth to a first-class production is hard to describe.

To save money and provide "involvement opportunity" to members of the community, you utilize a group of volunteer, unpaid assistants (really "errand persons or "go-fors"). In return for free admission to shows, they do whatever needs to be done: setting up tables and chairs, running errands, washing dishes, helping with props—whatever is needed at the time.

Since tickets for many of the productions are rather expensive, the assistant job is very popular. You have a large backlog of applications for it. Unfortunately, by its very nature, the work of assistants cannot be scheduled, so they often spend a lot of time sitting and waiting to be utilized. Typically, when they are needed, it's right then, and peaks in demand come unexpectedly.

One of the assistants, bright and able *Sandy Betts*, is more effective in action than most. S/he has a lot of savvy about how to do things quickly and effectively. However, Sandy strikes you as being somewhat of an irritating smart-ass. S/he acts superior to the other assistants and does not seem to respect the system and your needs. For example, the other night several assistants complained to you that Sandy was often not around when things got quite active and everyone was really needed; that s/he would be away visiting with people or just goofing off.

Later that evening, you were under the gun and up to your ears in unexpected delays and other problems. You had an urgent assignment for an assistant and none was available.

Recalling the comments about Sandy, you were pretty ticked-off. Finally, you tracked Sandy down at the bandstand. You had to rush away to another matter, but in giving her the assignment, you delivered a warning message loud and clear: "The other assistants are complaining about you, Sandy. Keep in mind that you can be easily replaced."

***The complaints have continued so you have sent word for Sandy to come to your office.***

***Have your* Learning Points Refresher Card *before you, and mentally rehearse what you will do.***

***When you are ready, start the roleplay.***

## Appendix C

# Rolesets for Three-Person Groups

## ROLESET FOR GROUP MEMBER T

### EXERCISE INSTRUCTIONS

*Important:* You will play the roles of "supervisor," "subordinate," and "observer" in four roleplay rounds that deal will an individual performance problem. To enhance realism, and help you to get the most from your practice, ***do not look at each other's rolesets until after the roleplay practice.***

The sequence of events for your first practice session is as follows:

1. In a prepractice meeting of all trainees, your Instructor will invite questions and discussion about the learning points.
2. As you watch a live demonstration or videotaped roleplay, you will be asked to check on a *Learning Points Worksheet* whenever any learning points occur. Then, your Instructor will invite you to compare notes with other group members as to where and when they occur and discuss any discrepancies.
3. You will go to your assigned group and place for roleplay practice, during which, your Instructor (or an Instructor Assistant) will visit your group to check on progress and answer any questions.
4. After roleplay practice, all groups will reconvene with the Instructor for comments, questions, and further instructions.

In one round, you will play the role of Supervisor; in another, the role of Subordinate; and in the other, the role of Observer. Study the requirements of each role carefully. ***Each of you will gain the most, if all of you are well prepared for all three roles.***

The information provided has been kept relatively simple and limited, so that your primary focus can be on implementing the learning points. ***Do not read important events into your role; for example, do not assume a bad past relationship, or that a strike has occurred, if such information is not explicitly mentioned.***

Study your supervisory role in this roleset. Think about how you might use the learning points in dealing with your "subordinate" in the roleplay. They should not be used mechanically—they are "tools" to apply with understanding and discretion, utilizing your own personal style. As a reminder, have the *Learning Points Refresher Sheet* before you when it is your turn to be Supervisor.

Study your role as Subordinate. Imagine the feelings this person might have, and practice expressing them before the roleplay.

Study the requirements of your role as Observer on the *Observer Form* (that you will fill in as you observe a roleplay). ***It is very important that you follow the three, post-roleplay steps in the sequence presented.***

### FIRST ROUND

***Your Role (Supervisor):*** Your name is *Robin Smith.* Three months ago you were appointed plant manager of an electronics firm that is coping with strong international competition and fast-changing technology and products. Previously, the company made lower-tech, standard products, and the demands on management and the workforce were more predictable and less challenging than they are now. You employ about 150 skilled and semiskilled workers who report to seven supervisors. You were one of these supervisors before being promoted.

Prior to the promotion, you knew that one of the average-performing, peer supervisors, *Carol Young* (now your subordinate), had begun to perform at a below-satisfactory level when the company shifted to its present, higher-tech activity. You had hoped and expected that Carol's unit would have gotten up to speed by now, but this hasn't happened. This assessment is based on *objective data* which permit direct comparisons with other departments that have the same resources in relation to workload.

From your knowledge and observations of Carol, you think that s/he has the technical knowledge and experience to be a good manager. However, you have observed that Carol:

- schedules new work poorly,
- is viewed as being cool and aloof by subordinates,
- has started coercing workers to put in unexpected overtime,
- fails to keep you informed of problems until they become crises (as s/he did with your predecessor).

Carol is currently your key problem. As far as you know, s/he has no serious personal, physical, mental, financial, or family problems.

Your other supervisors are doing an excellent job; in fact, you have been commended by headquarters for the manner in which the plant has performed and adapted to new demands. However, adaptation to the new conditions has been difficult for all of the supervisors in varying degrees, and you know that Carol is well-liked by them and has their sympathy.

***You have asked Carol to stop by your office to see you. Have your* Learning Points Refresher Card *before you, and mentally rehearse what you will do.***

***When you are ready, start the roleplay.***

## Second Round

***(Subordinate):*** Your name is *Chris Neely*. You have been a head nurse for a long time; in fact, lately you've felt it has been too long. You have lost interest in supervising others and in things in general. You have the feeling that everything is uphill and sort of hopeless.

You used to be a very competent head nurse. Now, supervisory responsibilities cause you to be anxious to the point that you have trouble sleeping at night. You find it difficult to make decisions that you once found easy to make. And you have become even more concerned and anxious since you promised your supervisor, *Jerry Brown*, several weeks ago that you would make every effort to improve. Yet, since then, you have actually gotten worse. Your group is now very low in both objectively measured performance and morale.

You would like to get out of your present job, but to do what? The way things are going, you wonder if you could handle an ordinary nurse's job until you are eligible to retire in 3 years. Given your nontransferable retirement credits, you would lose too much by leaving the hospital now. You live alone, have no one to turn to, and have no alternative assets to live on. Your retirement payments and social security will be just adequate.

Given your many years of good, faithful service, you feel strongly that it would be quite unfair if they try to throw you out in the street. In fact, if they do, you will appeal to some influential doctors on the medical staff whom you know well and think owe you for past accommodations you have made.

***Your supervisor, Jerry Brown, has called you in for a talk and you feel very apprehensive.***

## Third Round

***Your Role (Observer):*** Consult your *Observer Form* for instructions. The roles you will observe (as given to the roleplayers) are:

***(Supervisor):*** Your name is *Lane Thomas*. You were recently promoted from the payroll office of a textile mill to the position of maintenance supervisor. You supervise the maintenance workers who keep the machines going. You have had no training or experience with maintenance work, but since this involved an increase in status, pay, and visibility, you accepted it.

In giving you this new position, your boss reminded you that foreign competition is giving the company a hard time and that it is absolutely essential to cut costs to the bone. As he put it, "Maintenance expense is a nonproductive, but necessary evil; don't get any fancy ideas."

The other maintenance workers regard *Jo James* as one of the best of your crew. They say s/he is an outstanding diagnostician, works with amazing speed, and works hard. But you wonder. It seems that an increasing number of machines that Jo has just "fixed" break down soon after her intervention.

Could it be that her reputation with the other maintenance people is due to her likability, and that her good standing with the operators is based on "quick fixes" rather than on less superficial and more lasting repairs? (Quick fixes would minimize their downtime and lost potential earnings).

In an attempt to keep it light while communicating a subtle hint about the matter, on several occasions involving very short-lived repairs, you observed to Jo that "the machines must be afraid of him/her, because they have a nervous breakdown shortly after they see him/her." You're not sure that s/he took this with good humor.

In any event, the "hint" hasn't done any good, because two more recent repairs just went bad. ***You think it time to devote more attention to this problem and have asked Jo James to come by your office when s/he is free.***

***(Subordinate):*** Your name is *Jo James*. You are a highly skilled and experienced maintenance worker in a textile mill who fixes machines for the production workers. You pride yourself on your outstanding diagnostic and repair abilities. It makes you feel good when you are able to get the machines going again quickly, so that the operators will not lose potential earnings due to downtime (they are on a piece-rate, incentive-pay system, and many of them have become personal friends through the years).

Your new boss, *Lane Thomas*, was transferred from the payroll office and has had no experience with maintenance work. On several occasions, s/he has observed that an increasing number of machines break down shortly after you repair them. S/he made some kind of crack about "the machines evidently being afraid of you because they're having nervous breakdowns." Perhaps s/he was trying to be funny, but you're not sure, and you feel somewhat put out with this kind of "humor."

Fact is, the likelihood of breakdown has increased significantly as the machines have aged, and this is not your fault. You can't do justice to both preventive maintenance (regular disassembly, inspection, replacement of excessively worn parts, etc.) and the provision of prompt service that operators have come to expect. Actually, providing such prompt service has become even harder as the breakdown frequency has increased. And in your view, the basic problem is that management has failed to plan and budget for a needed preventive maintenance program; a need that was quite predictable. Of course, if they want to buy new machines, you won't mind a bit.

Your new boss's comments make you wonder if you and your hard work are really appreciated. You like the company and find your job challenging and rewarding. You would like to see the problem solved, but not at your expense. As a matter of fact, you can easily get a job elsewhere if you want to. ***Two more machines you recently repaired have just broken down and Lane Thomas has requested that you come to his/her office as soon as you are free.***

## Roleset for Group Member U

### Exercise Instructions

***Important:*** You will play the roles of "supervisor," "subordinate," and "observer" in four roleplay rounds that deal will an individual performance problem. To enhance realism, and help you to get the most from your practice, ***do not look at each other's rolesets until after the roleplay practice.***

The sequence of events for your first practice session is as follows:

1. In a prepractice meeting of all trainees, your Instructor will invite questions and discussion about the learning points.
2. As you watch a live demonstration or videotaped roleplay, you will be asked to check on a *Learning Points Worksheet* whenever any learning points occur. Then, your Instructor will invite you to compare notes with other group members as to where and when they occur and discuss any discrepancies.
3. You will go to your assigned group and place for roleplay practice, during which, your Instructor (or an Instructor Assistant) will visit your group to check on progress and answer any questions.
4. After roleplay practice, all groups will reconvene with the Instructor for comments, questions, and further instructions.

In one round, you will play the role of Supervisor; in another, the role of Subordinate; and in the other, the role of Observer. Study the requirements of each role carefully. ***Each of you will gain the most, if all of you are well prepared for all three roles.***

The information provided has been kept relatively simple and limited, so that your primary focus can be on implementing the learning points. ***Do not read important events into your role; for example, do not assume a bad past relationship, or that a strike has occurred, if such information is not explicitly mentioned.***

Study your supervisory role in this roleset. Think about how you might use the learning points in dealing with your "subordinate" in the roleplay. They should not be used mechanically—they are "tools" to apply with understanding and discretion, utilizing your own personal style. As a reminder, have the *Learning Points Refresher Sheet* before you when it is your turn to be Supervisor.

Study your role as Subordinate. Imagine the feelings this person might have, and practice expressing them before the roleplay.

Study the requirements of your role as Observer on the *Observer Form* (that you will fill in as you observe a roleplay). ***It is very important that you follow the three, postroleplay steps in the sequence presented.***

#### First Round

***Your Role (Observer):*** Consult your *Observer Form* for instructions. The roles you will observe (as given to the roleplayers) are:

***(Supervisor):*** Your name is *Robin Smith*. Three months ago you were appointed plant manager of an electronics firm that is coping with strong international competition and fast-changing technology and products. Previously, the company made lower-tech, standard products, and the demands on management and the workforce were more predictable and less challenging than they are now. You employ about 150 skilled and semiskilled workers who report to seven supervisors. You were one of these supervisors before being promoted.

Prior to the promotion, you knew that one of the average-performing peer supervisors, *Carol Young* (now your subordinate), had begun to perform at a below-satisfactory level when the company shifted to its present higher-tech activity. You had hoped and expected that Carol's unit would have gotten up to speed by now, but this hasn't happened. This assessment is based on *objective data* which permit direct comparisons with other departments that have the same resources in relation to workload.

From your knowledge and observations of Carol, you think that s/he has the technical knowledge and experience to be a good manager. However, you have observed that Carol:

- schedules new work poorly,
- is viewed as being cool and aloof by subordinates,
- has started coercing workers to put in unexpected overtime,
- fails to keep you informed of problems until they become crises (as s/he did with your predecessor).

Carol is currently your key problem. As far as you know, s/he has no serious personal physical, mental, financial, or family problems.

Your other supervisors are doing an excellent job; in fact, you have been commended by headquarters for the manner in which the plant has performed and adapted to new demands.

However, adaptation to the new conditions has been difficult for all of the supervisors in varying degrees, and you know that Carol is well-liked by them and has their sympathy. ***You have asked Carol to stop by your office to see you.***

***(Subordinate):*** Your name is *Carol Young*. You are one of seven supervisors of skilled and semiskilled workers in an electronics firm that is currently coping with strong international competition and fast-changing technology and products. You have been a supervisor for 9 years and are well-liked by the other supervisors.

Previously, when the company made lower-tech, standard products, the demands on management and the workforce were more predictable and less challenging than they are now. *Robin Smith*, a former fellow supervisor, was promoted to the position of plant manager (your boss) 3 months ago. S/he has been quite busy consolidating the plant's new mode of operation, so you've had little contact since the promotion. However, as far as you know, your relationship with him/her is okay.

You miss the greater stability and orderliness of the former mode of operating. For example, you've never been too keen about scheduling work, but at least under the old system things would tend to shake out after a little trial and error. But this has not worked too well under the new setup and the productivity of your unit has suffered. You are hesitant about asking the other less-senior supervisors for help, so you've tried to compensate for your errors by pushing your people for unexpected overtime. They don't want it and resent you for coercing them.

So, things are not going too well and the productivity of your unit, as revealed by objective comparisons with the other units that have essentially the same resources, has suffered. However, you have always believed that people should stay in their place and that they are expected to know what they are doing. Consequently, you maintain your distance from you subordinates, and you dislike troubling your boss about problems unless they really get out of hand.

During the last 3 years, there were two plant managers before Robin. They didn't seem interested in you as a person. They just kept pushing you to get your unit's output above the average level. You saw little reason for busting your butt for something you couldn't accomplish, and you weren't at all confident you would be fairly rewarded for significant increases.

***Robin Smith has asked you to drop by for a chat and you expect to get the same speech that you got from the former plant managers: that you have the technical knowledge and experience to be a better manager, but have the wrong attitude.***

## Second Round

***Your Role (Supervisor):*** Your name is *Jerry Brown*. You are the supervisor of a group of head nurses and you have just about exhausted your patience with one of them, *Chris Neely*. Chris used to be quite competent, but has fallen down on the job in the last 2 months. S/he puts off making important decisions, is increasingly neglectful of routine reports and duties, and seems generally unenthusiastic about his/her job. In fact, Chris's group is one of the least productive, based on several objective performance measures.

When you discussed Chris's deteriorating performance with him/her 3 weeks ago, s/he promised quite sincerely to do better. However, there has been no improvement and the morale among his/her nurses is low. Could it be that Chris thinks that long service has its entitlements, since s/he is just 3 years from retirement and knows that the hospital prides itself on looking after long-service employees? Maybe Chris thinks s/he can coast because s/he has some influential friends on the medical staff?

Chris lives alone and, as far as you know, has no other resources to live on. However, you cannot have a double standard for your head nurses. If necessary, you are now ready to consider termination.

***You have called Chris in for a talk.***

*Have your* **Learning Points Refresher Card** *before you, and mentally rehearse what you will do.*

*When you are ready, start the roleplay.*

### THIRD ROUND

***Your Role (Subordinate):*** Your name is *Jo James*. You are a highly skilled and experienced maintenance worker in a textile mill who fixes machines for the production workers. You pride yourself on your outstanding diagnostic and repair abilities. It makes you feel good when you are able to get the machines going again quickly, so that the operators will not lose potential earnings due to downtime (they are on a piece-rate, incentive-pay system, and many of them have become personal friends through the years).

Your new boss, *Lane Thomas*, was transferred from the payroll office and has had no experience with maintenance work. On several occasions, s/he has observed that an increasing number of machines break down shortly after you repair them. S/he made some kind of crack about "the machines evidently being afraid of you because they're having nervous breakdowns." Perhaps s/he was trying to be funny, but you're not sure, and you feel somewhat put out with this kind of "humor."

Fact is, the likelihood of breakdown has increased significantly as the machines have aged, and this is not your fault. You can't do justice to both preventive maintenance (regular disassembly, inspection, replacement of excessively worn parts, etc.) and the provision of prompt service that operators have come to expect. Actually, providing such prompt service has become even harder as the breakdown frequency has increased. And, in your view, the basic problem is that management has failed to plan and budget for a needed preventive maintenance program; a need that was quite predictable. Of course, if they want to buy new machines, you won't mind a bit.

Your new boss's comments make you wonder if you and your hard work are really appreciated. You like the company and find your job challenging and rewarding. You would like to see the problem solved, but not at your expense. As a matter of fact, you can easily get a job elsewhere if you want to. ***Two more machines you recently repaired have just broken down and Lane Thomas has requested that you come to his office as soon as you are free.***

## ROLESET FOR GROUP MEMBER V

### EXERCISE INSTRUCTIONS

***Important:*** You will play the roles of "supervisor," "subordinate," and "observer" in four roleplay rounds that deal will an individual performance problem. To enhance realism, and help you to get the most from your practice, ***do not look at each other's rolesets until after the roleplay practice.***

The sequence of events for your first practice session is as follows:

1. In a prepractice meeting of all trainees, your Instructor will invite questions and discussion about the learning points.
2. As you watch a live demonstration or videotaped roleplay, you will be asked to check on a *Learning Points Worksheet* whenever any learning points occur. Then, your Instructor will invite you to compare notes with other group members as to where and when they occur and discuss any discrepancies.
3. You will go to your assigned group and place for roleplay practice, during which, your Instructor (or an Instructor Assistant) will visit your group to check on progress and answer any questions.
4. After roleplay practice, all groups will reconvene with the Instructor for comments, questions, and further instructions.

In one round, you will play the role of Supervisor; in another, the role of Subordinate; and in the other, the role of Observer. Study the requirements of each role carefully. ***Each of you will gain the most, if all of you are well prepared for all three roles.***

The information provided has been kept relatively simple and limited, so that your primary focus can be on implementing the learning points. ***Do not read important events into your role; for example, do not assume a bad past relationship, or that a strike has occurred, if such information is not explicitly mentioned.***

Study your supervisory role in this roleset. Think about how you might use the learning points in dealing with your "subordinate" in the roleplay. They should not be used mechanically—they are "tools" to apply with understanding and discretion, utilizing your own personal style. As a reminder, have the *Learning Points Refresher Sheet* before you when it is your turn to be Supervisor.

Study your role as Subordinate. Imagine the feelings this person might have, and practice expressing them before the roleplay.

Study the requirements of your role as Observer on the *Observer Form* (that you will fill in as you observe a roleplay). ***It is very important that you follow the three, post-roleplay steps in the sequence presented.***

## First Round

***Your Role (Subordinate):*** Your name is *Carol Young*. You are one of seven supervisors of skilled and semi-skilled workers in an electronics firm that is currently coping with strong international competition and fast-changing technology and products. You have been a supervisor for 9 years and are well-liked by the other supervisors.

Previously, when the company made lower-tech, standard products, the demands on management and the workforce were more predictable and less challenging than they are now. *Robin Smith*, a former fellow supervisor, was promoted to the position of plant manager (your boss) 3 months ago. S/he has been quite busy consolidating the plant's new mode of operation, so you've had little contact since the promotion. However, as far as you know, your relationship with him/her is okay.

You miss the greater stability and orderliness of the former mode of operating. For example, you've never been too keen about scheduling work, but at least under the old system things would tend to shake out after a little trial and error. But this has not worked too well under the new setup and the productivity of your unit has suffered. You are hesitant about asking the other less-senior supervisors for help, so you've tried to compensate for your errors by pushing your people for unexpected overtime. They don't want it and resent you for coercing them.

So, things are not going too well and the productivity of your unit, as revealed by objective comparisons with the other units that have essentially the same resources, has suffered. However, you have always believed that people should stay in their place and that they are expected to know what they are doing. Consequently, you maintain your distance from your subordinates and you dislike troubling your boss about problems unless they really get out of hand.

During the last 3 years, there were two plant managers before Robin. They didn't seem interested in you as a person. They just kept pushing you to get your unit's output above the average level. You saw little reason for busting your butt for something you couldn't accomplish, and you weren't at all confident you would be fairly rewarded for significant increases. ***Robin Smith has asked you to drop by for a chat and you expect to get the same speech that you got from the former plant managers: that you have the technical knowledge and experience to be a better manager, but have the wrong attitude.***

## Second Round

***Your Role (Observer):*** Consult your Observer Form for instructions. The roles you will observe (as given to the roleplayers) are:

***(Supervisor):*** Your name is *Jerry Brown*. You are the supervisor of a group of head nurses and you have just about exhausted your patience with one of them, *Chris Neely*. Chris used to be quite competent, but has fallen down on the job in the last 2 months. S/he puts off making important decisions, is increasingly neglectful of routine reports and duties, and seems generally unenthusiastic about his/her job. In fact, Chris's group is one of the least productive, based on several objective performance measures.

When you discussed Chris's deteriorating performance with him 3 weeks ago, s/he promised quite sincerely to do better. However, there has been no improvement and the morale among his/her nurses is low. Could it be that Chris thinks that long service has its entitlements, since he is just 3 years from retirement and knows that the hospital prides itself on looking after long-service employees? Maybe Chris thinks s/he can coast because s/he has some influential friends on the medical staff?

Chris lives alone and, as far as you know, has no other resources to live on. However, you cannot have a double standard for your head nurses. If necessary, you are now ready to consider termination. ***You have called Chris in for a talk.***

***(Subordinate):*** Your name is *Chris Neely*. You have been a head nurse for a long time; in fact, lately you've felt it has been too long. You have lost interest in supervising others and in things in general. You have the feeling that everything is uphill and sort of hopeless.

You used to be a very competent head nurse. Now, supervisory responsibilities cause you to be anxious to the point that you have trouble sleeping at night. You find it difficult to make decisions that you once found easy to make. And you have become even more concerned and anxious since you promised your supervisor, Jerry Brown, several weeks ago that you would make every effort to improve. Yet, since then you have actually gotten worse. Your group is now very low in both objectively measured performance and morale.

You would like to get out of your present job, but to do what? The way things are going, you wonder if you could handle an ordinary nurse's job until you are eligible to retire in 3 years. Given your nontransferable retirement credits, you would lose too much by leaving the hospital now. You live alone, have no one to turn to, and have no alternative assets to live on. Your retirement payments and social security will be just adequate.

Given your many years of good, faithful service, you feel strongly that it would be quite unfair if they try to throw you out in the street. In fact, if they do, you will appeal to some influential doctors on the medical staff whom you know well and think owe you for past accommodations you have made.

***Your supervisor, Jerry Brown, has called you in for a talk and you feel very apprehensive.***

## Third Round

***Your Role (Supervisor):*** Your name is *Lane Thomas*. You were recently promoted from the payroll office of a textile mill to the position of maintenance supervisor. You supervise the maintenance workers who keep the machines going. You have had no training or experience with maintenance work, but since this involved an increase in status, pay, and visibility, you accepted it.

In giving you this new position, your boss reminded you that foreign competition is giving the company a hard time and that it is absolutely essential to cut costs to the bone. As he put it, "Maintenance expense is a nonproductive, but necessary evil; don't get any fancy ideas."

The other maintenance workers regard *Jo James* as one of the best of your crew. They say s/he is an outstanding diagnostician, works with amazing speed, and works hard. But you wonder. It seems that an increasing number of machines that Jo has just "fixed" break down soon after his/her intervention.

Could it be that his/her reputation with the other maintenance people is due to his/her likability, and that his/her good standing with the operators is based on "quick fixes" rather than on less superficial and more lasting repairs? (Quick fixes would minimize their downtime and lost potential earnings.)

In an attempt to keep it light while communicating a subtle hint about the matter, on several occasions involving very short-lived repairs, you observed to Jo that "the machines must be afraid of him/her, because they have a nervous breakdown shortly after they see him/her." You're not sure that s/he took this with good humor.

In any event, the "hint" hasn't done any good, because two more recent repairs just went bad. ***You think it time to devote more attention to this problem and have asked Jo James to come by your office when s/he is free.***

*Have your* **Learning Points Refresher Card** *before you, and mentally rehearse what you will do.*

*When you are ready, start the roleplay.*

Printed in the United States
136336LV00001B/2/P

9 781593 119812